Online Instruction

PRACTICAL GUIDES FOR LIBRARIANS

About the Series

This innovative series written and edited for librarians by librarians provides authoritative, practical information and guidance on a wide spectrum of library processes and operations.

Books in the series are focused, describing practical and innovative solutions to a problem facing today's librarian and delivering step-by-step guidance for planning, creating, implementing, managing, and evaluating a wide range of services and programs.

The books are aimed at beginning and intermediate librarians needing basic instruction/guidance in a specific subject and at experienced librarians who need to gain knowledge in a new area or guidance in implementing a new program/service.

About the Series Editor

The **Practical Guides for Librarians** series was conceived and edited by M. Sandra Wood, MLS, MBA, AHIP, FMLA, Librarian Emerita, Penn State University Libraries from 2014 to 2017.

M. Sandra Wood was a librarian at the George T. Harrell Library, the Milton S. Hershey Medical Center, College of Medicine, Pennsylvania State University in Hershey for over thirty-five years, specializing in reference, educational, and database services. Ms. Wood received an MLS from Indiana University and an MBA from the University of Maryland. She is a fellow of the Medical Library Association and served as a member of MLA's Board of Directors from 1991 to 1995.

Ellyssa Kroski assumed editorial responsibilities for the series beginning in 2017. She is the director of Information Technology at the New York Law Institute as well as an award-winning editor and author of thirty-six books, including *Law Librarianship in the Digital Age* for which she won the AALL's 2014 Joseph L. Andrews Legal Literature Award. Her ten-book technology series, *The Tech Set*, won the ALA's Best Book in Library Literature Award in 2011. Ms. Kroski is a librarian, an adjunct faculty member at Drexel and San Jose State University, and an international conference speaker. She won the 2017 Library Hi Tech Award from the ALA/LITA for her long-term contributions in the area of Library and Information Science technology and its application. Ellyssa left the series in 2021.

The series is now edited by Rowman & Littlefield Senior Executive Editor Charles Harmon, who was a librarian before entering publishing.

Recent books in the series include:

Online Instruction
A Practical Guide
for Librarians

Emily Mroczek

PRACTICAL GUIDES FOR LIBRARIANS, NO. 78

ROWMAN & LITTLEFIELD
Lanham • Boulder • New York • London

Published by Rowman & Littlefield
An imprint of The Rowman & Littlefield Publishing Group, Inc.
4501 Forbes Boulevard, Suite 200, Lanham, Maryland 20706
www.rowman.com

86-90 Paul Street, London EC2A 4NE

British Library Cataloguing in Publication Information Available

Library of Congress Cataloging-in-Publication Data

Names: Mroczek, Emily, 1990- author.
Title: Online instruction : a practical guide for librarians / Emily
    Mroczek.
Description: Lanham, Maryland : Rowman & Littlefield, 2022. | Series:
    Practical guides for librarians ; 78 | Includes bibliographical
    references and index.
Identifiers: LCCN 2021061711 (print) | LCCN 2021061712 (ebook) | ISBN
    9781538157671 (paperback) | ISBN 9781538157688 (epub)
Subjects: LCSH: Libraries and distance education. | Web-based
    instruction—Design. | Web-based instruction—Evaluation. | Information
    literacy—Web-based instruction. | Library education—Web-based
    instruction.
Classification: LCC Z718.85 .M76 2022 (print) | LCC Z718.85 (ebook) | DDC
    025.5—dc23/eng/20220106
LC record available at https://lccn.loc.gov/2021061711
LC ebook record available at https://lccn.loc.gov/2021061712

For my mom, who saw this book's beginning but not the completion.
Thanks for always supporting me.

And to all the friendly and knowledgeable members of Team Awesome,
past, present, and future. Keep changing lives for the better.

Contents

List of Figures

List of Tables

Acknowledgments

Thanks to all my family members and friends who believed in me, entertained my children, and offered support from near and far, especially my husband, Marek.

Thanks to Ellyssa for getting me started and to Charles and Erinn for their patience and guidance.

Thank you to all the library professionals who contributed their time and knowledge to this book: Heidi Fowler, Jenn Wigle, Michael Golrick, Paul Addis, Julia Frederick, Elizabeth Brown-Vaughan, Melanie Taylor Coombs, Janie L. Hermann, Leah Holloway, Lisa Mulvenna, Juana M. Flores, Julie Zimmerman, Chelsea Corso, Lisa Jones, Melanie Leivers, Emily Hampston, Carrie S. Banks, Christina Giovanelli Caputo, Marcia Keyser, Meghan Kowalski, Frank Skornia, Lisa Huelle, Stephanie Dietrich, Amanda Duntx, Dominique Hallett, Saran Silbaugh, Melody Friedenthal, Michael EcEvoy, Mary Martin, Amanda Jones, Sharon Fox, Heather Hedderman, Nicole Lawton, Ann Lautner, Tina Marie Maes, Kate-Lynn Brown, and Cristina Rapisardi.

Preface

Librarians have been working as online instructors since the Internet began. Libraries are a place where people can access technology and receive guidance about how to use digital resources.

Most libraries shut down when the COVID-19 pandemic hit the United States in March 2020. Librarians of all types turned into online instructors overnight. The transition was easier for some than others. Online instruction appeared in many forms, but librarians figured out technology to serve their communities. I watched many librarians struggle with the transition, lose sight of their purpose and become intimidated and overwhelmed by the digital environment. This handbook helps you get past the emergency philosophy and into the new normal.

Now, as the world attempts to navigate the new normal, it's important that we don't rush back to the way things were. Librarians of all types must evaluate what we learned from the pandemic and how we can use these skills to benefit our customers.

I've found the majority of how-to guides focus specifically on teaching in schools or adjusting to working at home, and many library online instruction books focus specifically on design. This book focuses broadly on the various types of librarians and online instruction, from public libraries to K–12 classrooms to universities to special libraries. The label may vary from virtual programming to online instruction to digital reference to hybrid programming; the audiences can range from typical students and patrons to people three countries away.

I wrote this book to empower librarians to instruct online and to easier navigate this digital world.

My graduate school assistantship involved working as a technical assistant in online courses at the University of Illinois at Urbana Champaign and setting up technology programming and documentation at the help desk. Half of my master's degree courses were online, and as part of one of them, I designed two computer labs for low-income families. These experiences guided me throughout my career, and I gravitated toward technology and helping others with technology whether in a special library (the Giamatti Research Center at the National Baseball Hall of Fame and Museum) or a public library (the Cincinnati and Hamilton County Public Library) and in day-to-day life. Many of my experiences come from places of privilege. Not all these ideas are feasible for everyone, but I hope they inspire you.

Online Instruction is encompassing for a broad spectrum of librarians, with areas that may be of more benefit to specific specialty areas. Feel free to skim this book and use the information that serves you best. The text operates on the assumption that you have basic knowledge of computers, Internet, and instruction but also covers the basics to help librarians navigate the digital world and give informed information to administration. This book serves as a starting point for further research and helps frontline staff and stakeholders decide many aspects of online instruction.

Because of the broad scope of this book, the language is also wide-ranging. The terms "how-to teach online," "digital librarianship," or "online instruction" can seem beyond your reach, but here, any type of online librarianship or instruction with others qualifies as teaching online. Examples include a formal class, open office hours, a story time, hosting a program, doing a live demonstration, or any other ways librarians may serve their community. I use the term "instructor" to signify the person leading a presentation; "participants" or "attendees" to mean students, patrons, community, or customers; and "institution" for an organization, university, library, school, or employer.

Transitioning from a physical learning environment to a virtual or hybrid environment does not need to be a loss, but an adjustment. The purpose of sharing knowledge or entertainment remains the same, and the technology is simply a vehicle. Online programs are constantly getting updated and reevaluated, which also happens with an in-person environment.

Librarians must adapt to the changing times and help their audience be comfortable with the changes. As online programs and models are constantly changing, this book will never be completely up-to-date, but the principles and ideas will help guide online instructors. *Online Instruction: A Practical Guide for Librarians* takes readers through the many facets of online instruction and issues that may come up specifically in libraries.

Recurring Themes

I repeat many themes, throughout this book, and although these may seem obvious, the themes are fundamental and important for any librarian taking on online instruction.

- *Content and information come first, technology comes after.* Don't let the technology take away from the content.
- *Technical difficulties are going to happen.* Things go wrong in both in-person and digital environments. Technical difficulties are inevitable, and what matters is how you deal with the problems.
- *Listen to your administration.* Many administrations control decisions for online learning. Always follow your organization's policies. However, don't be afraid to make educated suggestions that can better the situation for yourself, your staff, and your community. Remember that policies constantly change. Reference your institution's policies and consult your institution's legal counsel when needed.
- *Don't reinvent the wheel.* Many librarians and people in other careers are doing similar projects so you don't need to start from scratch. Find or create a community of practice that you can turn to for ideas and guidance. Just be sure to credit people for their work and to share and spread your own experiences.

- *We are all human.* This is uncharted water for many administrators, learners, instructors, and families. Do your best to have grace and patience with others as well as yourself.
- *Virtual programs are not going anywhere.* The surge of virtual programming began at the onset of the COVID-19 pandemic. That does not mean virtual programming should end with the pandemic. It is accessible, friendly, and important and is here to stay.

⊚ Organization

Online Instruction: A Practical Guide for Librarians has eleven chapters that cover various facets of online instruction. Feel free to skip to chapters that focus on the specific information you need. You may already know some information, and other sections may not apply to you.

Chapter 1 focuses on the history and purposes of online teaching along with the basics of getting started. Chapter 2 looks at pedagogy and thought process and how instruction styles translate into the virtual environment. Chapter 3 discusses creating set policies and behaviors, and chapter 4 covers the nuts and bolts of running a program. Building community—something that is extremely difficult, yet important—is the theme of chapter 5. Chapter 6 focuses on the pros and cons of various popular platforms, while chapter 7 breaks down the inner workings of Zoom, which many libraries are using. Chapter 8 looks at different types of digital resources and how to find quality options. Copyright, an important topic everywhere and especially online, is the focus of chapter 9, while accessibility, also important, is the center of chapter 10. In the conclusion, chapter 11, everything comes together with the goal that all readers can feel comfortable before leading any form of online instruction.

I hope that *Online Instruction: A Practical Guide for Librarians* will help you become comfortable in this virtual world. There are so many options out there and it is crucial to find what works best for you and your organization. Everything listed is simply a suggestion. You may have a better idea and that is okay. Plan and prepare as much as you can, but remember that we are all human and that technology has a mind of its own. No matter what happens in the future, digital instruction is not going anywhere. And librarians need to be ready.

CHAPTER 1

Online Instruction
Background and Getting Started

E-LEARNING, ALSO KNOWN AS ELECTRONIC LEARNING, is a broad definition of instruction through online means. Online instruction is equivalent to a traditional course environment, an individual program or training session, professional development, a learning module, or beyond. The fluidity of online instruction shows in the broad job description of librarians. It is up to individual organizations to determine their definition of online instruction and what levels of strategy and collaboration can make it successful for the instructors and user base.

Research and common knowledge show that quality instruction rests on the same foundations no matter the format—in-person or online. Virtual instruction presents a new set of challenges and demands because it expects different responsibilities for students and instructors besides the typical ones of learners and facilitators. A great deal of preparation is necessary for successful online teaching. It can prove difficult to accommodate varying learning styles. Clear and concise communication is important in the digital environment but is more difficult than in face-to-face instruction. Successful online teaching starts with a clear channel of communication between all stakeholders:

students, teachers, administration, and technology support. I've found that overpreparing and overcommunicating is cumbersome, but the best way to ensure that everyone is on the same page.

The various forms of online instruction include:

Synchronous: Virtual courses, webinars, and discussion groups, all live and in real time.

Asynchronous: Modules, discussion forums, tutorials, or videos where learners participate at their own pace and time, where people learn at different paces.

Blended learning: A combination of synchronous and asynchronous work where participants have assignments and forums in between live sessions or some days online and others in person.

Hybrid learning: Asynchronous courses or sessions where some learners attend live and others virtually.

Self-led: Similar to asynchronous, digitally posted courses where students don't report to an instructor but simply access video, audio, and print content and participate at their own pace.

Social learning networks: Twitter chats, Facebook Live events, and Instagram and TikTok stories are all ways social networks work for online education and to build communities of practice.

Virtual communities: Discussion forums and public or private social networking groups are grounds for digital learning communities. ALA Connect is the main communication for the American Library Association and subgroups.

One-on-One Education: Mentoring, tutoring, and coaching can take place over video chat services, social networks, or email.

Distance learning: Similar to correspondence learning, people fill out packets, then receive feedback from instructors. This form of learning is applicable to all ages with packets and print resources.

Libraries are a very versatile field, and instruction takes different directions depending on the specific library.

Online degree programs and continuing education: Many library science programs and other college programs have online tracks with either self-paced modules or live sessions. Students and staff interact through emails, web conferencing, social networking, and online learning management systems (LMS).

Elementary school, junior high, and high school: Some K–12 elementary schools had distance education before COVID-19, with most US schools transferring digitally in March 2020. Education took place through synchronous and asynchronous learning, with live sessions on streaming services like Zoom or Webex and districts using learning management systems like Moodle, Google Classroom, and Seesaw. As restrictions eased up, many schools transferred to hybrid and blended learning formats.

Preschool and early childhood education: Preschool programs, music classes, nature classes, and library story time are available online. Programs for the younger age group often have movement and music on livestreaming devices, YouTube videos, or resources geared toward parents.

Conferences: Professional development and online conferences are often digital, using a combination of webinars on YouTube, Zoom, or other services, communication through conference website and email list servers, and recorded videos sent to attendees.

Adult programs: Libraries, museums, and other organizations moved many programs to a digital format. Individuals pick up supplies at the organization and then attend a live demonstration. Book groups and other clubs meet synchronously with a central hub for resources between meetings.

In addition to the various purposes for online instruction, libraries have varying focuses depending on their purpose.

Academic and research libraries: Academic and research libraries are often available for affiliated students and faculty, along with community or alumni classes. These feature topics or information around a specialized topic.

Public libraries: Public libraries serve the taxpaying community and also neighboring libraries or other people who may find need for their services. Individuals are often looking for access to resources, a physical space, or entertainment.

School libraries: K–12 school libraries primarily serve the learning needs of their students along with student teachers, caregivers, administrators, and teaching assistants.

Corporate libraries: Corporate libraries' user bases consist primarily of company employees and at times other private organizations.

Miscellaneous special libraries: The glossary of various special libraries is vast, with many specialized libraries serving specific needs and interests, including but not limited to hospital and prison libraries, law libraries, and theological libraries.

Digital Instruction Is the New Normal

Teaching and instruction are not always taught in library school, but are a part of many library jobs, whether in a formal course, through public programming, or in a one-on-one format. During COVID-19, most library programs, meetings, training, and conferences moved online, and librarians became online instructors overnight. Figure 1.1 is a word cloud created during a virtual programming presentation I hosted in March 2021. The prompt for participants was "What words come to mind when you hear the term virtual programming?" The answers ranged from "Zoom, Internet, and computer fatigue" to "engagement" to "no engagement" to "more possibilities."

As the world moves into the "new normal," online education is not going anywhere. Hybrid and online-only options are going to be the standard as they allow for better flexibility and can reach a larger number of people. Many companies have updated policies to allow for at least a partial work-from-home environment, or even transitioned into completely remote companies. Though a key part of libraries remains the physical space, the public is going to continue expecting remote options. The flexibility of attending courses virtually and accessibility of watching videos on one's own time make online education very appealing for many learners of all ages.

On a personal level, as a young mom, I find it much easier to attend library programs from home. My husband and I enjoy attending adult programs while the kids are sleeping. We would not normally attend these events if they were in person.

Figure 1.1. Virtual programming word cloud. *Emily Mroczek, Mentimeter*

History of Online Education

Distance learning and online education have many different origin stories to go along with their fluid definitions. We can credit distance education to beginning in the late nineteenth century with correspondence study through the postal service. Multimedia distance education began with one-way technologies, including radio and televised broadcasts.[1] Distance education really took off in the beginning of the twenty-first century.

The Open University of the United Kingdom formed in 1969, with the first students taking courses in 1972. Desmond Keegan's definition of distance education came out in 1972, with six elements including:[2]

- the separation of teacher and student
- influence of an educational organization
- use of technical media
- two-way communication
- seminars
- participants

In 1986, the American Center for the Study of Distance Education began at Penn State, where a small group of educators explored how to extend educational access through distance education. The next year, the United States Distance Learning Association (USDLA) began, the first nonprofit organization for distance learning research. In the 1990s and early 2000s, online courses started at a variety of universities worldwide.

The University of Phoenix launched a fully online college with bachelor's and master's degrees in 1989, and in 1996 Glen Jones and Bernard Luskin launched Jones International University, the first accredited web-based university.[3] In 2008 massive open online courses (MOOC's) emerged, which provided open access to content, learning goals, and courses with unlimited use.

Melanie Leivers, children's librarian for a public library in Minnesota, did the majority of her bachelor's and master's education online in the early 2000s. "Although it doesn't work for everybody, it is in no way a new platform to complete classes and programs. Mostly all of the program was online and did not have 'in person' alternatives," Leivers said. "Instead, there would be lab hours to receive help as needed. I have always thrived more in online learning than in-person learning."

During the COVID-19 pandemic, most educational and recreational programs were canceled or moved online. This forever transformed education and training as the forced closure of schools required mandatory distance learning, even if participants and instructors were not prepared. As stated by Victor García-Morales et al., "The current scenario has involved a rapid pedagogical shift from traditional to online class sessions, personal to virtual instruction, and seminars to webinars."[4]

Throughout these events, libraries served and supplemented online learning and instruction and provided a physical space or equipment, instruction, or tutorials. The mission of libraries will continue to evolve alongside constantly changing technology.

Benefits and Challenges of Online Instruction

For some users, the benefits of online education can be drawbacks and vice versa. The truth is that each individual learner is different and there will be pros and cons to every decision, and all these factors should require consideration when determining session formats.

Benefits

Digital learning saves time, materials, and physical space. Physical rooms don't need reservations and specific setup. Attendees and instructors do not need to commute to a class or lesson. We can update resources and textbooks easier in a digital format than in print.

Technology is constantly becoming more accessible. Many people can access free programs and implement the new products into their events and curriculums. Content can be virtually infinite if your attendees have digital access. Recording sessions provide the opportunity for attendees to pause, transcribe, and slow down recordings. These features can aid special-needs learners, those for whom English is a second language, and struggling readers. Materials from online courses are easier to archive because of the technical capabilities and cloud features of digital programs.

Online teaching opens new doors. Participants can attend sessions from any geographic location. Not having to commute opens new opportunities for guest speakers, for presenters from around the world, and for visiting different places one may never get an opportunity to physically explore.

E-learning provides a comforting and relaxed environment. Virtual learning has less pressure than in-person education and welcomes more non-traditional learners. Participation and interaction can be less intimidating thanks to multiple avenues available for responses including reactions, polls, and chat.

Collaboration possibilities increase. Libraries and organizations can network together from around the world. Libraries can combine resources and events rather than having to choose one library's physical location.

Speakers can come from anywhere. Guest speakers and presenters can enter presentations virtually, which would not be feasible in a face-to-face environment. Fees on hotels, food, and airfare are nonexistent.

Hybrid options boast the best of both worlds. With hybrid options, programs can reach people craving both an in-person and digital experience. This expands reach and accessibility.

Challenges

Connectivity can be problematic. Not everyone may have the equipment, technology, or knowledge to attend online classes. These barriers need addressing, and solutions need to be present for all users to have access to learning opportunities. There is the constant possibility that technology crashes and simply cannot work. Many online education programs are not accessible or are limited when using a smartphone.

There can be a lack of separation. Being able to attend classes remotely can make it difficult for people to take time off for vacations, personal appointments, or mental health.

The online scene is constantly evolving. Programs receive constant updates, copyright permissions change, and new technology comes out. This issue makes it difficult to find concrete evidence and statistics for what methods work best. Just when you think you conquered the latest technology tool, a new one comes out. The constant addition of faster and better tools are overwhelming. Sticking to one tool is helpful, and only test out something new if you feel comfortable and ready.

Technology does not come naturally to everyone. For some, transferring a session or class to a virtual format can be seamless, while for others the mere prospective is daunting. Technology tools and best practices may be a specialty for technology administrators but not instructors and learners. Also, students may be at a similar intellectual level but different technical level.

Online education can have more no-shows, lower completion rates, and lower attention spans. These drawbacks carry weight when making a decision for an in-person or virtual session and also when deciding what to have registrants invest in the lesson.

Monitoring pieces of the class can prove overwhelming. It can be difficult for one person to monitor all the aspects of a program from sign-ups and technology issues to questions and participant issues. A way to avoid this problem is through an additional instructor or aide, which could present a staffing issue.

Focus and engagement can be difficult. At home, distractions and physical separation can make monitoring participation quite difficult.

The challenges of traditional instruction still exist. In addition to all of the above challenges, one still has to deal with the traditional challenges educators and instructors have dealt with for years: varying administrations, learners, and everyday distractions.

More than half the battle of online education is planning: deciding on technology, how to use it, and how to teach it to participants. An organization may already have policies in place, major decisions made, and interfaces created. Other decisions will be entirely up to you. The combination of restrictions and freedom can be a mix of exhilarating and overwhelming. This chapter will help you get started and help evaluate your needs through self-reflection.

TEXTBOX 1.1

Leah Holloway, a public relations assistant at the Augusta–Richmond County Public Library System in Augusta, Georgia, shares her experiences with virtual programming and maintaining it at her library.

"This whole experience has taught me that virtual programming is here to stay, and every library should be finding ways to incorporate it into its systems. We are still doing some virtual programming for those who may still be wary of coming to the library though we have returned to having in-person events over the past couple of months. We just had a mostly virtual Star Wars Reads event for the second year in a row. Future directions may include recording and/or livestreaming some of our in-person programs. We will also continue to use the software for promotional purposes. We will continue to establish a positive digital space for our audience. Some people refuse to come out, and we always want to have options available to them for programming and events."

Examine Your Boundaries

The vast options and possibilities in online education can seem overwhelming. That's where administration guidelines are helpful. Take a look at what decisions and policies your organization has in place and use that as a starting point. If you did not receive any policies and procedures about online instruction, ask. You don't want to plan everything out and then have to start over. Make sure you have a clear focus on goals (skills the group is working toward over a designated time), skills (proficiency), and strategies (step-by-step guides) as you plan your session.

Questions to ask:

How does offering online instruction support your library's overall mission and vision?

How much time, budget, staff expertise, and other resources can your organization offer to online instruction?

How does the chain of command work at your organization? Who is responsible for what aspects of online programming?

Where should instruction take place?

What equipment is available for staff members and attendees? What are staff members required to provide?

What streaming services does your organization currently use? Are additional services available to use or request?

What digital subscriptions does your organization currently subscribe to? Are you able to request additional subscriptions?

What policies or rules exist about attendees, copyrights, and other issues?

What training, assistance, and technical support does your organization offer?

What specific support is available before, during, and after your sessions?

What features must you have and what can you live without?

Evaluate Your Skills

Be realistic about your goals and capabilities as an instructor. Remember that pedagogy and content come first and technology comes after. Chapter 2 discusses digital pedagogies and their importance in the online environment. Don't get so lost in the bells and whistles that you forget who you are as an instructor.

In any format, a quality presenter needs to grasp the audience's attention, engage a variety of learners, deliver a message, and be clear and concise. Maintaining attention can be difficult when you cannot see your attendees. Use technology to enhance learning and to incorporate instructional design and teaching skills into a digital environment.

It is easy to think that you have no experience with online instruction. Think about everything you've participated in and what skills you gained from those activities.

In this self-evaluation, think about your own relational abilities, communication styles, compassion, persistence, and empathy and how those characteristics can transfer to the digital environment. Remember that just as the more you teach a topic, the more you know about it, the more you instruct online, the more fine-tuned and experienced you become.

Self-reflection questions:

What experience do I have in online instruction (either formal or informal)?

What type of digital environment do I thrive in?

What livestreaming and LMS systems have I used before?

What am I most excited about and nervous about with online instruction?

What resources are in place to help me (organization resources, professional organizations, personal networks)?

◎ Programming Types

Once you know your purpose and audience, you can make more informed decisions about the programming types and interfaces. Goals should include how to best showcase your content and be user-friendly.

TEXTBOX 1.2   FORMS OF PROGRAMMING

- One-off: A lecture, story time, seminar, workshop, or class that is a stand-alone program. No prior or future attendance is necessary, even if it is a repeating event.
- Series: An event with multiple sessions that feed off one another. Learners do not complete work in-between sessions.
- Group/club/class: Something that takes place over an extended period of time and has multiple formats for learning and communication.

Another key decision about programming types is whether you are hoping for a synchronous or asynchronous environment. Synchronous uses real-time interaction, individual and group work, presentations, input from community, shared resource tools, and activity monitoring. This form of teaching mixes presentation of material, problem-solving, quizzes or games, and group work. For some learners, the similarity to an online classroom works best. This environment provides more room for technical errors and additional assistance is needed from support staff or parents. Individuals complete synchronous learning in their own time through a learning management system or other central hub. Participants may view videos, blog posts, or web pages and post discussion questions and answers but do so on their own timeline. Interaction takes place during a set time.

Audiences differ depending on age, purpose, interests, background demographics, and technology proficiencies. Purposes for online learning include entertainment, formal or informal education, and socialization.

A helpful trick is to list computer skills needed for a specific program (for example, word processor use, spreadsheet capabilities, how to save and download files). More information about planning programming is available in chapters 3 and 4.

Types of technology proficiencies include those who grew up with digital media, those introduced to the Internet in high school or college, those who adapted and are comfortable with digital technology, those who only use technology on an as-needed basis, and those who have limited to no experience with technology. Self-reflection questions:

What type of program are you leading?

Who is your primary audience?

What is the purpose of your program?

If there is an in-person program that you are trying to replicate, what aspects work in the digital format?

How do you want to connect with your audience?

Will you treat your audience more as passive attendees or active contributors?

Establish Your Platform and Resources

Chapter 6 outlines details of specific learning management systems, videoconferencing services, and livestreaming options. We will also take a precursory look at the plethora of online resources available. Try to not overdo digital resources and only use what can truly supplement the content.

Also, an institution may have a preexisting contract with a medium. Often, these agreements apply to the larger platforms you are using, while supplemental videos and resources are up to the instructor. Chapter 6 also discusses reasoning to add or change platforms, despite complicated red tape.

Equipment and Setup

Once you have your platform and plan, it's crucial to make sure you have the proper equipment for a quality program. Think about your personal equipment and technology but also that of your attendees. Practice with equipment and technology and to always have a backup plan.

Equipment is one of the most important parts of digital programming. Technology failures are going to happen. The most you can do is put yourself in the best situation possible. It is also important to invest in quality equipment that you know will work. Ideally, your organization will support these equipment requests because an investment in equipment matters, but it could also be helpful to have personal equipment.

Designated space: Whether you are in an office, at home, or both, it's important to have a designated space for online instruction. This space helps create a comfortable presence for you and your attendees. If a space is not working for you, try to identify and fix the problem. Think about switching where items are or where equipment lives. Headphones, apps, or a white-noise machine can help block out background noise or other distractions.

A dedicated space doesn't have to be a full room and can be a shared space that's used for a similar purpose. Our video recording room at my old library had a table, frequently used story time supplies, a green screen and lights, and a flannel board. Not having to move this equipment every time made recording a lot easier.

For better web quality, it might be beneficial to go to a library or public place to do an online session. However, public places may have additional background noise, ever-changing hours, and conference rooms with limited availability.

Recording equipment: Depending on your needs, it may be easier to record using a standard smartphone or tablet, or a laptop. You need additional capabilities depending on the project. Tripods or a base can lead to steadier footage. Explore different devices to determine their limits and your comfort level.

Connection: A stable Internet connection is key. Wired is best, or wireless with a high broadband connection. Boosters are available to help a connection. Wireless hotspots are available on cellular devices or as individual entities and can be helpful backups.

Hardware: Effective hardware is the starting point for a successful virtual program. Audio is most important. If you lose video, class can still go on, but if you lose your audio, you cannot teach.

A quality computer that runs fast can help manage the equipment you are using. A second monitor can be useful to open and view all of your tabs. Laptops have a great deal of flexibility and are ideal for distance learning environments, but desktops are more budget-friendly and better for ergonomics. It is ideal to hook a laptop up to an external monitor.

Examine your computer for the necessary ports and cords for any add-ons. Most computers have built-in webcams, but others don't, and fewer and fewer laptops have CD drives, Ethernet ports, or even USB drives. If you want any peripherals like an external monitor, keyboard, mouse, or scanner, make sure it is compatible with your device.

Most devices come with adequate microphones, but test it out for quality. Getting your own microphone and headset can help localize sound. It is important to always select the correct microphone from your audio lists to ensure the audio goes through. It is helpful to have a backup for all your equipment in case anything breaks down. An HD camera is key for quality. Most come with the computer, but Logitech makes quality add-ons.

One of my biggest programming fails was when I did not have video for an entire program because I forgot to open the webcam lens on a desktop computer. I was able to engage because of the sound, but it was still unfortunate.

Software: Make sure that your device is up-to-date and compatible with any programs you are using. Word processors, web browsers, plug-ins, anti-virus programs, and pop-up blockers vary depending on software. Remember to check all plug-ins and updates well before a program begins, to prevent any last-minute software changes or updates.

Lighting and visual: Good lighting helps a presenter look professional and focused. Eliminate any bright lights behind you, close the blinds, turn off lamps, and reposition cameras. It can be helpful to buy a ring light to adjust lighting levels.

Choose a visually appealing but not distracting background. Wearing neutral clothes is less distracting during presentations. The best camera position is at eye level, which avoids any awkward angles and conveys a level playing field with your audience. Standing desks can be helpful to achieve eye level, as can propping your device on books and boxes, using a tripod, or purchasing an adjustable device holder.

Chelsea Corso, a children's librarian at the Barrett Paradise Friendly Library in Cresco, Pennsylvania, recommends testing eequipment multiple times. "Shadows, lighting, and audio can all change depending on the time," Corso says. "Things can also change from device to device, and it is always good to have a backup device."

Participant equipment: Think about what equipment to recommend for your participants. What is required for the best experience? Are there any minimal capabilities?

Depending on your institution, you may require, recommend, or provide certain equipment. No matter what, you should try to determine the general types of technology your audience has. This knowledge can help you make an informed decision about what platforms to use. You can do a questionnaire at registration to survey participants' technologies. Some institutions provide devices for attendees. Once you know what devices your participants are using, you can confirm if your platform is compatible.

Security: If filming from home, try to blur your background or go somewhere that does not give off any personal details. I did an egg-drop video from outside my apartment building and blurred out the street address in all the clips so no one could identify my location. Remember when screen-sharing to close any unrelated tabs or image to avoid potential embarrassment or unprofessionalism.

When asking for participation, be aware of privacy and security. It is tempting to require videos on or full names, but a person may have a reason for keeping their camera off or their last name private. All participants must be notified if a session is recorded. Determine your organization's privacy policies and make sure you are aware of public versus private information.

Ergonomics: Working at computers all day can be difficult on the body, and key ergonomics and equipment will help you in the long run. Many companies have employee wellness programs with helpful information and budgets for wrist wrests, anti-glare screens, and quality computer chairs. Practice solid posture, where you sit back with your head and neck straight and have your feet touch the floor.

Cloud storage: Digital files and resources need a host location. Options include a library web page or institution's storage through Google Drive, Amazon Drive, Microsoft One Drive, or Apple iCloud. Table 1.1 compares various popular cloud storage options.

I use flash drives to store specific videos that I don't need for a current project but can quickly access. I also back up my files on an external hard drive, but that is harder for me personally to access and keep up with.

Instructor Roles

In a digital environment the instructor picks up a lot of additional responsibility. In addition to the typical content expert and crowd management, a presenter becomes:

- an in-between with student and institution to provide information and advice
- a learning mediator
- a technical assistant with enough technical skills to intervene with the system and resolve limitations on attendees
- an adaptor who can present content and materials in a way that favors learning with the device at hand
- an engaging and interactive speaker in a digital environment
- able to adopt a number of aids to meet multiple learners' needs

As shown in table 1.2, a virtual program has all the same goals as in-person, with additional responsibilities and pressure. All of these additional roles are workable, but instructors need the necessary time and energy to give the task justice.

Figure 1.2. An ergonomically friendly workspace. *Marek Mroczek*

Table 1.1 Cloud Storage Options

NAME	EMPHASIS	FREE STORAGE	KEY NOTES
Google Drive	File storage, sharing, and collaboration	15 GB	Comes with Gmail account
Microsoft OneDrive	Functionality with Office applications	15 GB	Comes with company Microsoft packages
Apple iCloud	For Apple users	5 GB	Family sharing across Apple products
Dropbox	Simplicity, ease of use	2 GB	Integrates with third-party services
IDrive	Backup	5 GB, yearly fee	Works well with multiple devices

Table 1.2 In-Person versus Virtual Programming

FOCUS	IN-PERSON PROGRAMMING	VIRTUAL PROGRAMMING
Who	Individuals in your user base	Individuals in your user base and around the world
What	Story times, book clubs, classes, outreach	Story times, book clubs, classes, outreach
Where	Library or classroom	Library, classroom, or your home, reaching everywhere
When	Wednesdays at 7 p.m.	Wednesdays at 7 p.m. and beyond
Why	To promote literacy	To promote literacy
How	In-person event, done one time	Digital event, possibly also in-person, possibly recorded and edited for future use

Create a Plan

Organizations should have guidelines in place for digital programming, especially if they want to abide by certain standards and have consistency. Scripts can help maintain consistency for programs, along with parameters about filming locations, length of time, and common practices. A guide should include any necessary feedback survey, metric counting, or other ways to measure program success. Individual states may have guidelines for tracking virtual program attendance. Evaluate programming decisions through an equity, diversity, and inclusion lens to ensure differing populations receive support.

Schedules and deadlines also help everyone stay on track. System-wide decisions about copyright are also critical so that everyone in the organization is on the same page. Clear and concise expectations and procedures will make implementation of programming run smoother and staff more open to assist with online programming.

ⓖ Key Points

- Online instruction takes several forms and definitions but essentially is using technology as the primary vehicle for education.
- With constantly improving digital technologies and a need for accessibility, online education is not going anywhere.
- Challenges of online instruction can also be benefits, and benefits may have challenges as well. Individual teachers and learners need to find what works for them, similar to a traditional classroom.
- Determine your expectations and abilities for online instruction along with the mission and policies for digital instruction, equipment, and technology.
- Planning is key to a quality program.

ⓖ Notes

1. Jennifer Sumner, "Serving the System: A Critical History of Distance Education," *Open Learning: The Journal of Open, Distance and e-Learning* 15, no. 3 (2000): pp. 267–285, https://doi.org/10.1080/713688409.

2. "Distance Education Timeline," American Center for the Study of Distance Education, accessed June 24, 2021, https://sites.psu.edu/acde/2019/02/02/distance-education-timeline/.

3. "The Evolution of Distance Learning," Florida National University, August 15, 2019, www.fnu.edu/evolution-distance-learning/.

4. Víctor J. García-Morales, Aurora Garrido-Moreno, and Rodrigo Martín-Rojas, "The Transformation of Higher Education After the Covid Disruption: Emerging Challenges in an Online Learning Scenario," *Frontiers*, February 11, 2021, www.frontiersin.org/articles/10.3389/fpsyg.2021.616059/full.

Pedagogical Matters

THE MERRIAM-WEBSTER DICTIONARY defines pedagogy as the art science, or profession of teaching. I think of pedagogy as what guides an instructor from the core as a teacher and a learner. There are many pedagogical concepts and theories out there and they all stand at the base of instruction, even in technology. The key is to find ways the pedagogies transfer into the digital environment without losing your instructional style. This chapter is a brief overview of popular pedagogies with ideas for using them digitally. It is an not a substitution for individual research on learning theories.

Transferring Pedagogy

Despite the differences between online teaching and the traditional classroom style, the pedagogical learning foundations remain the same. It is important to remember to place pedagogy first and technology second. Digital tools can help support and address different thinking skills, however, it is important to not let the lesson or purpose get lost in the ocean of technology.

Passwords, logins, and fancy applications can take away from the actual content and relationships. Sometimes I get so excited about the technology that I lose focus on the lesson at hand. A concept I like to think about is the $1,000 pencil, where people apply new tools to do old work when what was needed was to redesign the principles and thought process.[1]

Remember that many principles of pedagogy effective in an online classroom, video, simulation, and text are also effective in an in-person environment. Digital tools allow people to engage across multiple learning styles. You can apply pedagogical principles and tools to synchronous and asynchronous learning environments. When looking at your individual pedagogy, choose the best combination of resources and tools for yourself and your attendees.

Here is a basic look at popular teaching models and ideas to transfer them to online instruction.

Bloom's Taxonomy or Bloom's Digital Taxonomy (1956)

The main objectives of Bloom's Taxonomy are some of the most widely used in teaching. This model classifies levels of human cognition through thinking, learning, and understanding.

The original words of Bloom's Taxonomy pyramid are: knowledge, comprehension, application, analysis, synthesis, and evaluation. In adaptations of Bloom's model, the words changed to verbs, which are: remember, understand, apply, analyze, evaluate, and create. All of these concepts transfer easily over to a digital education, and digital tools can supplement the concepts.[2]

Create: Combine elements to form a functional whole. Make a blog, write a program, remix a musical score, edit a video, or record a podcast. Tools include: avatars, green screen applications, memes, photo and video editing programs, podcasts, and QR codes.

Evaluate: Judge based on criteria and standards through checks and critiques. Online grading, digital quiz, moderating, and discussion and feedback. Tools include: form builders, digital quizzes, automatic grading systems, polls and surveys, and discussion boards.

Analyze: Break concepts into parts and determine how they interrelate to one another. Mind mapping, surveying, linking, validating, estimating, and categorizing. Tools include: content curating, student portfolios, teacher tools, and whiteboards.

Apply: Use materials through models, diagrams, and presentations. Calculate, chart, edit, upload, construct, and experiment. Tools include: games, file sharing, presentations, screencasting, social networking, and word clouds.

Understand: Construct meaning from different types of functions. Bookmark, highlight, search, copy and save, summarize, predict, identify, and demonstrate. Tools include: graphics, virtual flash cards, virtual reality, critical-thinking tools, document sharing, online journals, and Twitter.

Remember: Use memory to produce information. Write a document, search for information, bookmark favorite sites, or list ideas. Tools include: word-processing systems, collaboration tools, blogging, and calendar and scheduling tools.

I outline many of the above tools in chapter 8, "Evaluating and Recommending Resources."

Maslow's Hierarchy of Learning Needs (1943)

Maslow's theory rests on the idea that human beings have certain hierarchical needs in order to learn. Starting at the lower levels and moving up, the needs are: physiological, safety, belonging, esteem, and self-actualization.[3]

Physiological needs cover an access to resources including access to power, wireless Internet, and basic technology devices. *Safety needs* mean account security and directional and informational access. Video chatting and social networking with personal networks are ways to meet the needs of *belonging* and love, while photo and video sharing systems can meet the needs of *esteem*. *Self-actualization* needs include promoting one's self works on networking sites like YouTube and LinkedIn.

Technology satisfied the hierarchy of needs during the COVID-19 pandemic. When most everyone stayed home, they looked to technology for connections, and creativity emerged. Now, librarians can take everything we learned during the pandemic to continue fostering connection and engagement through technology.

Constructivism

Adapted from many learning theorists, constructivist theory allows an active process of knowledge construction. Learners bring past experiences and cultural factors into the learning experience. This easily transfers into the digital format because many discussion-based models thrive on participants' past experiences.[4] Instructors who don't usually use the constructivism theory might try it in the online environment, where people are craving more connection.

Lave and Wenger Communities of Practice (1991)

Jean Lave and Etienne Wenger coined this term while looking at the learning model of apprenticeships, because a community acts as a living curriculum. The three characteristics of a community of practice are domain or common interest, community or shared activities, and practice (the community members participate in the community). Communities of practice can be very effective in a digital world, where people can connect to one another via social networks, massive online open courses (MOOCs), and small groups and breakouts from those networks.[5]

Presence and Relationships

The three types of classroom presence are social, teaching, and cognitive, as defined by the Garrison, Anderson, and Archer Community of Inquiry model. *Social* presence is the sense of being with one another, something difficult yet critical to achieve online. *Teaching* presence is the combination and design of social and cognitive presences to create a meaningful educational outcome. *Cognitive* presence is the quantity and quality of critical thinking.

Social Presence

Faculty and students achieve social presence by putting their individual characteristics into discussion and showing themselves for who they are.[6] Ways to model social presence include: sharing personal information about educational background, families, work experiences, or fun facts such as pets, favorite foods, or music to help build connections. Other fun ideas could be sharing a favorite vacation photo or a special memory.

Participant investment occurs if attendees feel connected to the instructor and one another. There could be features like "getting to know you" discussion postings, introduction time at the beginning of live sessions, special discussion threads for informal exchanges, or casual time for meeting and greeting before or after class. To fulfill this presence, it is important to establish a culture of respect and openness in your virtual space. Chapter 5 focuses entirely on building community and connectivity in the digital environment.

Teaching Presence

Teaching presence equals the amount of preparation done before and the work done during the time of a class. It includes having course materials prepared before the start date of instruction and being an active instructor throughout the entire period of the course. Preparation and active involvement are the best ways to create a strong teaching presence. A clear and concise course syllabus that states expectations and the system for announcements and changes can create a positive environment. Other ideas are an open channel of communication for one-on-one questions and comments and email, phone, or other private messaging tools. It is also key to obtain feedback through comments on forums, blogs, or Wiki pages.

Cognitive Presence

The definition of cognitive presence is "the extent to which the professor and students are able to construct and confirm meaning through sustained discourse (discussion) in a community of inquiry."[7]

Cognitive presence is very similar to social presence, but the focus is more on connections through beliefs, cultural influences, and thoughts. It is opening up one's mind to others. This action takes participation and effort from teachers and learners. It involves asking participants to share personal goals and ideas.

Ideas to foster a cognitive presence include creating open-ended assignments and discussion forums. It can also be helpful to create summaries of weekly discussions to focus on teaching and learning outcomes. Instructors should deeply examine student responses and use follow-up questions that encourage deeper thinking.

Employing these three practices can be key in building relationships with students. The instructor is a key model of participation. It can be difficult to connect with participants in a virtual environment, but these connections can be even more important to help determine students' needs.

Digital Pedagogies

Along with the traditional teaching pedagogies, unique digital best practices and pedagogies come into play. There are specific mind models that can work better online and practices that account for the change in medium and lack of in-person communication.

Chris Morgan and Meg O'Reilly wrote a book in 1999 called "Assessing Open and Distance Learners." The foundations and best practices Morgan and O'Reilly discuss still relate to today's virtual environment.[8] Some of their best practices include: a clear, rational, and consistent pedagogical approach; explicit values, aims, criteria, and standards; authentic and complete tasks; a facilitative sense of structure; sufficient and timely formative assessment; and awareness of the learning context and perceptions.

Another read specifically about multimedia is Richard Mayer's book *Multimedia Learning*, in which he looks at specific mind models[9] that work with online instruction. Some of his most helpful mind models are:

- Signaling: visually highlighting the most important points you want attendees to remember.
- Spatial contiguity: placing captions as close as graphics as possible, to decrease visual shifting between the two. If using diagrams, place captions next to the relevant parts of graphics instead of above or below the graphics.
- Temporal contiguity: placing spoken narration and graphics as close to one another as possible.
- Segmenting: breaking a presentation into several short segments.
- Pretraining: setting up a module for concepts and terminology before a presentation.
- Modality: People learn better from pictures and audio narration than pictures and text.

I find that many of Mayer's mind models transfer well to an in-person environment as well.

In 2007 the Association of College and Research Libraries (ACRL), a division of the American Library Association, established "Standards for Proficiencies for Instruction Librarians and Coordinators," outlining twelve specific categories of core skills for instruction librarians and coordinators.[10] The twelve categories are: administrative skills, assessment and evaluation skills, communication skills, curriculum knowledge, information literacy integration skills, instructional design skills, leadership skills, planning skills, presentation skills, promotion skills, subject expertise, and teaching skills. There are a total of forty-one core proficiencies for instruction librarians and twenty-eight additional ones for instruction coordinators. The entire guide is definitely worth a read. Below, I highlight six proficiencies that apply to the broad level of online instruction detailed in this book.

6.7. Integrates appropriate technology into instruction to support experiential and collaborative learning as well as to improve student receptiveness, comprehension, and retention of information.

6.8. Identifies, encourages, and supports training opportunities for librarians in instructional design and incorporating technology to support pedagogy.

8.1. Plans presentation content and delivery in advance, and manages preparation time for instruction.

9.2. Presents instructional content in diverse ways (written, oral, visual, online, or using presentation software), and selects appropriate delivery methods according to class needs.

9.3. Uses classroom instructional technologies and makes smooth transitions between technological tools.

12.3. Participates in constructive student-teacher exchanges by encouraging students to ask and answer questions by allowing adequate time, rephrasing questions, and asking probing or engaging questions.

A final theory that specifically highlights digital pedagogies is Lisa Guernsey's 3C's: context, content, and the child. This method applies to the early childhood and K–12 audience. *Context* looks at how presentation complements but does not interrupt natural play. *Content* looks at if the children can engage and express with the display. And *child* exemplifies choosing tools and lessons that balance and support children. The three C's focus on: learning, family engagement, and diverse needs. Although this concept is intended for children and family, it is applicable for all digital learners.

All the above theories highlight important ideas to keep in mind when designing and presenting online instruction. Remember that a lot of these ideas are common traits of librarians and we have been doing this work for our whole careers. Now we are simply transferring our resource sharing and strategies to the digital environment. It is important to pay more attention to supporting training opportunities and preparing content in advance, when there is more unknown and potential for technical difficulties.

Communication

In any form of education, but especially online instruction, communication is key and a part of most pedagogies. The lack of in-person relationships, many visual and vocal cues, and struggle for engagement can make teaching in the online classroom difficult. It is important to try to form a connection and build relationships with attendees, while still watching out for one's emotional well-being. When making the choices in designing your program, think about what methods are needed to communicate clearly to your participants and not to overwhelm them, yourself, or your administration. Specific strategies for communication engaging the audience are in chapter 5, "Building Community."

Active learning helps a digital learning environment become more interactive and engaging. Ideas are polls with live answers, visual quizzes, wikis the students can update, expert panels, role-playing activities, debates, group projects and breakout rooms, short video installments, and visual graphics.

Experimental learning may take place more online, where students learn by doing and reflect on the experience. This style can seem difficult in a virtual environment but is a great time to look back at creative immersive experiences offered in response to the COVID-19 pandemic. The ADDIE model also can help guide teaching analysis, design, development, implementation, and evaluation, which looks at instructional design.

It is key that an instructor finds a pedagogy that works best for them and their attendees. These pedagogies can differ from program to program and instructor to instructor. Observing other courses, looking at past recordings and soliciting feedback from students can all contribute to refining and developing the online teaching pedagogy. It is important to experiment and learn from experimentation.

Self-reflection questions:

What learning and teaching practices do you currently use?

What pedagogies guide your teaching?

Who is your target audience and what type of learners are they?

What kind of learning activities fit in with your learning outcomes, content, and the principles of learning in your class?

In looking at the above pedagogies and competencies, I find it important to point out that these are conversations librarians have had for years even if they don't have traditional titles of teacher or instructors. In their daily work, librarians construct knowledge and promote open content and reader engagement, and in doing so librarians contribute to digital learning. Think about what aspects you bring to your job daily as a librarian, to your instruction, and how you already use digital tools and knowledge to share that information with your user base.

Key Points

- Remember to place pedagogy first and technology second.
- Most pedagogies easily transfer to the digital environment with digital tools to supplement the pedagogy.
- Establishing social, teaching, and cognitive presences helps build a positive relationship with students.
- Look at how traditional pedagogies apply best practices for technology.
- Librarians have been employing many of these practices for years and are transferring them to the digital domain.

Further Reading

Brewer, Pam. "Pedagogical Perspectives for the Online Education Skeptic." *Journal on Excellence in College Teaching*, October 13, 2014.

"The Community of Inquiry Model." Community of Inquiry Model | Denver. Accessed October 27, 2021. https://operations.du.edu/inclusive-teaching/community-inquiry-model.

Donohue, Chip. *Technology and Digital Media in the Early Years: Tools for Teaching and Learning.* New York: Routledge, 2015.

Fowler, Clara, Carla Wilson Buss, Chad Kahl, and Susan Vega Garica. "Standards for Proficiencies for Instruction Librarians and Coordinators: A Practical Guide." American Library Association. Association of College and Research Libraries, June 24, 2007. www.ala.org/acrl/sites/ala.org.acrl/files/content/standards/profstandards.pdf.

Mayer, Richard E. *Multimedia Learning.* Cambridge, UK: Cambridge University Press, 2020.

Morgan, Chris, and Meg O'Reilly. *Assessing Open and Distance Learners.* London: Kogan Page, 1999.

Williams, Joseph Jay. "Applying Cognitive Science to Online Learning." *SSRN Electronic Journal*, 2013. https://doi.org/10.2139/ssrn.2535549.

Notes

1. Alan November, "Crafting a Vision for Empowered Learning and Teaching: Beyond the $1,000 Pencil," November Learning, November 5, 2018, https://novemberlearning.com/article/crafting-vision-empowered-learning-teaching-beyond-1000-pencil/.

2. Dr. Kecia Ray, "Updating Bloom's Taxonomy for Digital Learning," TechLearning Magazine (Tech & Learning, February 16, 2021), www.techlearning.com/news/updating-blooms-taxonomy-for-digital-learning.

3. Abraham H. Maslow, *A Theory of Human Motivation* (Radford, VA: Wilder Publications, 2018).

4. George E. Hein, in *Exploratorium*, accessed September 12, 2021, www.exploratorium.edu/education/ifi/constructivist-learning.

5. Etienne Wenger, *Communities of Practice: Learning, Meaning, and Identity* (Cambridge, UK: Cambridge University Press, 2018), 6–32.

6. D. Randy Garrison, Terry Anderson, and Walter Archer, "Critical Inquiry in a Text-Based Environment: Computer Conferencing in Higher Education," *The Internet and Higher Education* 2, no. 2–3 (1999): pp. 87–105, https://doi.org/10.1016/s1096-7516(00)00016-6.

7. D. Randy Garrison, Terry Anderson, and Walter Archer, "Critical Inquiry in a Text-Based Environment: Computer Conferencing in Higher Education," *The Internet and Higher Education* 2, no. 2–3 (1999): pp. 87–105, https://doi.org/10.1016/s1096-7516(00)00016-6.

8. Chris Morgan and Meg O'Reilly, *Assessing Open and Distance Learners* (London: Kogan Page, 1999).

9. Richard E. Mayer, *Multimedia Learning* (Cambridge, UK: Cambridge University Press, 2020).

10. Clara Fowler et al., "Standards for Proficiencies for Instruction Librarians and Coordinators: A Practical Guide," American Library Association (Association of College and Research Libraries, June 24, 2007), www.ala.org/acrl/sites/ala.org.acrl/files/content/standards/profstandards.pdf.

Policies and Procedures

SIMILAR TO ANY IN-PERSON LEARNING ENVIRONMENT, policies and procedures are necessary in an online environment. With a lack of physical space and a looser format, sometimes a "no rules" structure is tempting. But, a sense of calm and uniformity helps everything run smoothly. Create a plan—have all the information in one location to refer to. This central place prevents users from searching aimlessly for information.

Intentions and Expectations

As mentioned throughout this book, instructors are models of behavior and help provide user support.

Julie Zimmerman, a children's librarian at the Brooklyn Public Library in Brooklyn, New York, puts intention at the root of all digital programming. "I would say the two things I found most helpful have been: to set intentions and set expectations for the experience upfront," Zimmerman said. "I use a set of community agreements that are age-appropriate for my audience as well so that it feels like a safe space. Especially when working with children, I leave a little extra time for folks to answer so that everyone feels like they can participate if they want to. Maybe they can't find the button to unmute or maybe they're taking extra time to think. I want to give them that moment before rushing on to the next segment of the thing we're doing."

Try to make roles in the rooms clear for facilitators, participants, technology assistant coordinators, attendees, and any observers. Table 3.1 defines these roles. An understanding of everyone who is present builds a culture of respect.

Table 3.1   Roles in a Virtual Session

NAME OF ROLE	DUTIES
Instructor (Teacher)	Main person running the room and sharing knowledge
Presenter	Person sharing knowledge and information
Technical Assistant	Person helping with technical issues and monitoring the chat, waiting room, and beyond
Facilitator (Moderator)	Introduces the program, answers logistical questions, could also serve as Technical Assistant
Participants (Students, Attendees)	People attending the program
Observers	People shadowing the program

Communication is key, especially when it is harder to read tone and body cues. Model the communication you hope to receive: clear, concise, and professional (grammar), knowledgeable (concrete examples), substantive (speak with meaning), and respectful (polite). Remember that you are speaking with people from all over the world so remembering time zones and social differences is important.

You can't assume that someone already knows something unless it's a prerequisite. Try making guides or how-to videos for frequently asked questions. These resources keep information clear and concise and provide a location for attendees to reference.

On an instructor's end, try to enter a digital room a few minutes early to answer any questions, set ground rules for how you call on participants, limit screen sharing for easier visualization, and allow people to pass if they are uncomfortable speaking. Be sure to give extra time for technical difficulties and questions. People engage in a variety of online environments, so be gracious: They may not know the same general etiquette as you. Make your expectations clear for how you want messaging, participating, and cameras used while keeping privacy and personal needs in mind. If you are recording a session, make sure everyone receives notification.

General Digital Etiquette Practices

- Use cc and bcc appropriately—cc for the main recipient(s) of a message and bcc only when absolutely necessary.
- Before posting a new question or forum topic, read through postings and check if it already exists.
- Check your punctuation and avoid all capital letters and exclamation points unless you are trying to make a strong point.

- Keep your microphone off and muted when not speaking to avoid background noise (and potential embarrassment).

⑥ Participant Buy-In

One of the biggest drawbacks of online programming can be a lack of connection and interaction. Chapter 5, "Building Community," has many useful tips that can help participant buy-in. A lot of pressure falls to the instructor to ensure a participant's engagement in the program. It is easier for someone to exit a Zoom room than a physical room, or to forget to log on to an asynchronous class than skip an in-person program. Ideas for maintaining participant buy-in are creating fun and engaging experiences, modifying if a lesson isn't working, using technology that helps the program, and providing participants opportunities to interact with one another through conversation and group activities.

Talk to your attendees and find out what their purposes and intentions are: completion certificates; whether they're attending for enjoyment, out of obligation, or relevancy to real-life experiences. Knowing motivations and personal stories can help you make the session more fruitful.

Plan time at the beginning of a session to explain how things will work and what might be different to first time e-learners. It can be helpful to draw in your audience with a fun feature like a special speaker, digital poll, or virtual game.

If attendees feel like members of the community and are invested in it, they are more likely to return.

⑥ Staff Guidelines

Oftentimes, an organization has many staff members putting on programs and running classes. Although everyone has their own style, standard guidelines give instructors direction, make sure everyone is on the same page, and make it easier for substitutes.

Staff need guidelines and appropriate resources to ensure consistency and quality. These guidelines include program templates, examples, ability to shadow other programs, and standards for time and content. Staff also should have an understanding of important elements such as lighting, audio, frame, and attire. Providing staff with a script, or template syllabus, recommending a "system check" for technical issues, and having someone sit in on a virtual session are all ways to ensure consistency and quality. Balance is important though—if staff members feel there is no room for creativity, quality may suffer.

Susan Silbaugh, a children's librarian at the Willowick Public Library in Willowick, Ohio, likes having another person in her programs. "For instructing online successfully, I recommend having a buddy," Silbaugh said. "Jump on the program fifteen to twenty minutes early with your buddy, and test all the songs, links, stories, and whatever else you will be using. The buddy/co-host is so fantastic because if anything happens—Wi-Fi goes out, technology dies, etc.—they can carry on and finish the program. They are also there to keep an eye on chats and help patrons with any technical issues they may be having (or muting kids that are being too rowdy)."

◎ Attendance

Institutions need a policy for recording attendance. Options to track attendees are: page views, time spent viewing a video, or a poll for attendees. State libraries may have standards for tracking digital program attendance.

Attendance is difficult to measure and maintain during in-person and digital programs. When people struggle with digital numbers, I always remind them that not all in-person programs are consistently well attended either.

There's nothing fun about preparing the perfect program and then having no one show up. Remember that no-shows happen with in-person events too. Erin Weaver, assistant director at the Bridgeville Public Library in Bridgeville, Pennsylvania, said, "With online programs, you can usually expect about half of those who register to actually show up. Even with sending reminders out, that just seems to be the standard attendance rate."

Evaluate whether you advertised enough, what the timing was, and how you can get more attendees next time. And in the digital environment, it is crucial to make sure your attendees received the correct link.

As with many in-person classes and programs, wait a certain amount of time before a program cancellation. This time limit is a helpful inclusion to institutional policies.

◎ Security

Many users and instructors have apprehension about online programs because of potential security breaches. There are risks no matter the avenue, but you can make educated decisions and perform best practices to keep data and sessions as secure as possible. Make sure to follow organizational policies, enable a password for meetings, and only share the link with attendees. Also request that the link not be shared, and allow limited functions for participants.

Ask permission before recording any programs and before taking screenshots of a program. Organizations should be familiar with local, state, and federal privacy laws along with company privacy policies.

Programs for children under thirteen require additional restrictions. Most libraries are not themselves subject to the Children's Online Privacy Protection Act (COPPA), but must choose COPPA-compliant platforms. The Family Educational Rights and Privacy Act (FERPA) applies to all schools that receive funds under the US Department of Education and protects the privacy of student education records. The Children's Internet Protection Act (CIPA) requires schools to have an Internet safety policy to receive E-rate funding.

Screen sharing. A helpful tool that involves learners in real time, screen sharing could be a disaster. Turn off any message and chat notifications along with closing unnecessary windows to avoid potential embarrassments.

Platforms. Depending on your target audience, think about if you want people to be anonymous or create user accounts. Look for platforms with clear privacy, data use, and data retention policies. Trustworthy companies should make their policies clear. There's a big difference between using data to improve the user experience and selling data to make a profit. Investigate what happens to content after deletion.

Melody Friedenthal, public services librarian at the Worcester Public Library in Worcester, Massachusetts, values privacy in her programs. "Make sure your name, and not just your library's name, is displayed," Friedenthal said. "Take advantage of all the security options your platform allows."

Virtual programming introduces new questions about personally identifiable information, registration requirements, and focusing content depending on the audience.

⑥ Feedback

Feedback is not something that needs to wait until the end of an entire term, session, or program. There's immediate feedback in the moment: "Can everybody hear me? Can you see the screen okay? Are you in the correct room?" Reactions and chat can be helpful for immediate feedback, and polls work for informal feedback. Casual reflection at the end may also be beneficial. "Is there anything else you wanted to know? Would you benefit from any additional resources? What was the most confusing part of the session for you? Please email me or come to office hours if you have any questions or concerns." Asking for feedback after a program is very important to evaluate programming moving forward.

For formal courses, possible questions include: How were University Resources? Did online resources enhance the program? Would you take future online courses by this instructor? Did the instructor communicate effectively and timely? Did the instructor stimulate discussions and act professional?

Project Outcome is a free toolkit that provides sources for measuring and analyzing outcomes in public libraries, created by the Public Library Association.[1]

When measuring the impact of programs, views and attendees are important, but it's also key to dig deeper. Look at the analytics on social media, see how long people were watching a video, and look at comments. Download and share the comments, which can be great to add to testimonials.

Feedback is helpful to determine necessary changes before the next session and ensure participants are receiving value from the program. Evaluate all feedback and ensure that any large changes will benefit the group as a whole and that the cost and time benefit is worth it. Feedback can also be given to attendees to help reinforce concepts and make sure they are getting the most from the course.

One benefit of recordings and online learning is that instructors can watch their lessons and take note of any changes they want to make.

⑥ Technology Tips

Technology problems are going to happen. The Internet could break, microphones stop working, a server can overload, and the list goes on and on. There is no way to stop technology problems from happening, but there are ways to decrease the likelihood of them, to increase troubleshooting skills, and to improve everyone's attitude during difficult times.

A standard practice is, "unless the problem is something you can solve in fifteen seconds or less, don't try to solve your attendees' problems." Technology issues can be very distracting, and you don't want one participant's troubles to dominate the class. In an ideal situation there is a secondary person available to help with technical issues, or a person people could contact via their private chat or phone. Other troubleshooting options include having office hours to troubleshoot technology, or creating an FAQ sheet with tips and tricks. In case of technical issues, have a technical-difficulty slide you can display on-screen. Take a deep breath and remember that technology problems happen to everyone and that issues can happen in person too.

Frank Skornia, a digital librarian in Information & Adult Services at the Ferguson Library in Stamford, Connecticut, advises on prepping for technology issues.

> If you are used to doing in-person instruction, take time to examine your methods and identify what areas may need to be different in an online environment. Do not assume that everyone attending your instruction session will have the same technological proficiencies or resources, but also set a threshold of what is the lowest-level proficiency they should have to be able to take part and make that clear numerous times before and during the session. You should not spend a lot of time during the instruction session helping people to navigate your chosen platform's interface.

Make sure to teach your attendees how to use any platform, technology tool, or app. Send a video or instructions in advance, or volunteer to be available a little before the session. Make sure that your attendees know whom to reach out to so you can stay focused on instruction. These strategies prevent attendees from missing out in the moment, or taking time away from your session for explanations.

Troubleshooting Tips

Turn it on and off again. A simple reboot can help refresh connections, reset a program, and clear the memory. Also, log in and out, disconnect and reconnect all devices. However, do not simply pull the plug. Select "Shut down" or "Restart" from the Start menu, press CTRL+ALT+DEL twice, and if neither of those options works, then hold down the power button for about five to ten seconds. Wait about half a minute and try rebooting your device.

Check the basics. Sometimes there is an easy fix. Make sure all the cords are plugged in correctly, refresh all your windows, turn on your power strips, and check that your monitor is on. Check your wireless connection. Restart a router if necessary.

See if others are having difficulty. There might be larger server or power issue that has nothing to do with you. Reach out to others, check Twitter accounts, call a help line, or see if anything is in your email or anything else for the organization.

Recent changes. Think about what changed recently on your computer. Did you download any new software? Turn off a setting for another project? Add any new devices? Any of these could create an issue.

Possible Issues

A plug-in does not work. Go into the browser settings and clear the cache.

No one's here. If you're in a session but no one else is there, double-check that you clicked the right link. Try entering from a different direction. Check the time zone and any other relevant information and reach out to attendees.

Can't log in. Check that all your addresses and login information are correct. Make sure that you are on the right screen. Try opening the program from a new browser window.

Browser crashed again. If your browser keeps crashing, make sure the browser and program are current on updates and try a system reboot.

I hear loud noises. If you're hearing strange noises, try unplugging and plugging in your microphone and muting and unmuting your audio.

There's no sound. Verify the audio connections, reset connections by pressing mute and unmute, and ask everyone to plug in and re–plug in their headphones.

I submitted my assignment but it's not there. Always complete any assignment or discussion responses in a separate Word file and save it. Then, if it gets lost, you have a backup.

TEXTBOX 3.1

Melody Friedenthal, public services librarian at the Worcester Public Library in Worcester, Massachusetts, advises asking attendees to arrive early to avoid technical issues.

"Since you may have to individually allow access to each student to the virtual classroom, ask students to arrive at least five minutes early so you are not distracted by late arrivals and you can work out any technical difficulties that might arise."

Training

Along with staff policies, training is critical to ensure staff is ready to teach in a virtual environment. Even if a staff member has taught virtually before, it is helpful to learn about a company's specific procedures and the specific platform. If instructors receive proper training and support, they are more likely motivated to perform well.

"The key to successful online programming is gifted staff," Melanie Taylor Coombs, adult services supervisor and librarian at McArthur Library in Biddeford, Maine, said. "There is no doubt that our successful online programming came from dedicated individuals working together to implement ideas. Any platform can be a disaster in the wrong hands. Our most successful training and programming came from the brilliant minds of our team at McArthur Library."

Distractions

Distractions happen everywhere and especially online. In 2017 a live interview on BBC went viral.[2] Professor Robert Kelly was doing a live interview from his home office in South Korea when his toddler daughter and her baby brother strolled into the room, followed by his frantic wife. He took it in stride and carried on. This interview serves as a model for dealing with distractions and issues online.

Have a contingency plan in case something goes wrong, and have a backup plan for the contingency plan. But remember, there's only so much you can do.

Remind attendees that it's okay to turn their camera off if something is happening in their space. If an attendee is being distracting, the easiest option is to mute them. If the distraction continues, a technical assistant could move the individual to a breakout room and talk to them. If all else fails, there are options to remove an attendee from a room and continue the session.

⊚ Key Points

- Create organizational policies and procedures.
- Do what you can to protect security.
- Have a backup plan in case technology goes wrong.
- Communicate your system clearly to attendees and other instructors.

⊚ Further Reading

Hughes, Kathleen M., and Jamie Wirsbinski Santoro. *Pivoting during the Pandemic: Ideas for Serving Your Community Anytime, Anywhere.* Chicago: ALA Editions, 2021.

⊚ Notes

1. "Performance Measurement: Introduction to Project Outcome," Public Library Association (PLA), January 22, 2021, www.ala.org/pla/data/performancemeasurement.
2. "Prof Robert Kelly Is Back & This Time His Wife . . . ," YouTube, accessed September 1, 2021, www.youtube.com/watch?v=PLMSoD1riE0.

CHAPTER 4

General Programming

IN THIS CHAPTER

▷ What are the best practices for online instruction?

▷ What are the different types of library programs and what medium do they work best on?

▷ How can I run a smooth and successful digital program?

ONLINE TEACHING IS TRULY AN ART, where one learns through experience. You pick up tips and tricks along the way, and every lesson is a learning experience. Many parts of in-person programming transfer over online, but online instruction requires an additional level of coordination and creativity. Remember to not lose yourself in the gadgets, to face reality, and to ask for help. This chapter has ideas and brainstorming for running a program with the many pieces that go together. When brainstorming digital programming, think about past successes, ideas you always wanted to try, and your population's wants and needs.

Types of Programs

Programming Structures

Series vs. one-time classes vs. semester courses. Presenting a program as a series reaches a large number of people and accomodates those who have to miss one event. They also help generate a following. One-time events are helpful to gauge interest and not overuse resources. A full semester long course is ideal for required classwork or intensive training.

Asynchronous vs. synchronous learning. Synchronous (live) learning offers real-time feedback and interaction and immediate answers to questions. However, session quality depends on the individual instructor, one-on-one attention is difficult, and it adheres to a strict schedule. Asynchronous learning offers flexibility, expands reach, and saves money. But it may create a feeling of isolation, provide limited contact, and it requires a self-disciplined participant and instructor.

The iSchool at the University of Illinois at Urbana-Champaign was a pioneer of online learning. Online courses had asynchronous and synchronous aspects with one on-campus day a semester with an in-person class session. Students attended the on-campus days every semester of their degree program. This on-campus day ended in favor of a single Welcome Weekend, where new students received a three-day required orientation on campus structured like a mini conference.[1]

Micro learning. With the influx of social media and digital technologies, short videos, reels, and mini documentaries have gained in popularity. People want information, but they want it fast.

Low technology options. For people who may struggle with accessing technology, providing recordings on a flash drive, print packets, or materials and instructions are a way to reach them.

Hybrid. Hybrid options are popular in a "best of both worlds" approach. Individuals attend in person or online. Any program or class has the potential to transfer to hybrid, however, the impact may decrease.

Questions to ask about hybrid learning include:

Will a hybrid experience improve the situation for people? Is hybrid necessary? How can I maintain interaction and satisfaction from in-person and digital technologies?

Blended learning was most often done in schools during the COVID-19 pandemic, where students would spend several days learning remotely and the remaining days in the classroom.

Passive programming. Popular in libraries, programming done on one's own time is a way to reach a large number of people. Polls, surveys, and contests work as passive programs and can easily transfer to the online environment.

🌀 Specific Programs

Book Clubs

Book clubs meet to discuss literature. They easily transfer to a livestream model in a discussion or meeting approach, but also work as hybrid or using a passive learning environment like Goodreads, Facebook Groups, or a Slack channel.

Key questions: How will my audience best interact with one another? What platforms are my regular attendees comfortable with? Do I want an asynchronous or synchronous book club model, or a combination of both?

Digital integrations: For example, book clubs could meet synchronously at scheduled times and have an asynchronous hub for additional conversations.

Related program ideas: Round tables, social justice and current-events conversation groups, interfaith group discussions, virtual cafes on predetermined topics, mental health check-ins.

Webinars

Webinars are Internet seminars that have a large audience and don't require audience participation. People may attend live or watch a recording. Training programs, guest speakers, and one-off programs often flourish in a webinar format.

Key questions: How much do I want attendees to participate or ask questions? How many attendees do we anticipate? Is the webinar recorded? How many people need speaking privileges?

Digital integrations: Webinars integrate with many livestreaming and video applications.

Program ideas: Author talks, expert panels, and informative training sessions work well in the webinar format.

Story Times and Early Childhood Programs

Story times and early childhood programming are two of the most common programs in public libraries. Child programs are typically a stand-alone event but may recur on the same day and time every week. People may prioritize screen time and interactivity decisions depending on the specific age group.

Key questions: What privileges do I want the attendees to have? What level of interaction do I want with the attendees? What technology is my audience familiar with?

Figure 4.1. Toddler participating in virtual story time. *Emily Mroczek*

Additional ideas: Story-time kits could be available for pickup with books, props, and additional activities.

Related program ideas: Puppet shows, virtual play groups, music and movement, concerts, sing-alongs, process art.

School-Age Programs

Most programs that school-age children attend in real life can transfer to the digital format. However, some work better than others. STEAM programs, coding courses, and interactive activities can work best.

Key questions: What privacy and registration rules do we want with school-age kids? Would school-age kids benefit from hybrid programs?

Related program ideas: Character and book clubs, coding tutorials, cooking and sewing demonstrations.

Demonstrations

Cooking demonstrations, science projects, and various tutorials work well online. Options include a live and interactive audience or recording with a screen-capture program. People could pick up relevant materials from the library.

Questions to ask: What is the most important element of this program (seeing the content, following along, having instructions)? Would this work better live or recorded?

From the field: Paul Addis, a reference librarian at the Coos Bay Public Library in Coos Bay, Oregon, did a community cooking workshop with a co-op. "Some of the work I've recently done around this program via an ALA grant allowed for us to provide free ingredients," Addis said.

Meetings

Meetings are one of the most common forms of digital instruction. It is common to make meetings hybrid, with people attending in person and remotely. Digital meetings are helpful for public record and reference.

Additional ideas: Split meeting participants into breakout rooms for small-group discussions. Remember to give remote participants a chance to weigh in. Try to give out agendas and handouts in advance for extra preparation for attendees.

Key questions: How many people are attending this meeting? What features do we want to use?

One-on-One Instruction

Tutoring, office hours, and media help are all often done through one-on-one instruction. Video communication and screen sharing is a productive way to conduct business.

Questions to ask: What visual is most important? How long will the session take place? Is it a set time or flexible?

Related ideas: Performance reviews, parent-teacher conferences, and technical troubleshooting.

Recorded Videos

Oftentimes live meetings, training, or programs are recorded for later use and sometimes editing. These integrate onto websites or social media where people can watch on their own time.

Key questions: Is any of the video content confidential or copyright protected? Do I want the videos accessed in a closed or open format?

Social Media Networks Learning Networks

Facebook, Twitter, or other social media accounts reach various demographics. Videos, Instagram Reels, or photos promote conversation and engagement. Supplement posts between larger virtual programs to help keep patrons engaged and encourage frequent visits to your organization's social media platforms. Tie in learning tips and related library resources, and encourage patron participation through comments and hashtags to increase post impact. Many passive programs such as coloring pages, guessing games, and surveys transfer over easily to the digital environment, often through social media.

Questions to ask: What social network does my audience use most? Does my content belong on this social network? How can I modify preexisting content to fit on a specific network? How can I supplement programs on a social network and create social network–exclusive programs?

⑥ Transferring Activities

Many programs and activities transfer easily over to an online format. We should evaluate methods to make sure the technology enhances the content.

If showing content, look for items that translate well to the screen, like large books and props. Try to pick visually engaging and easily demonstrable activities. Think about necessary supplies for activities. Try to use commonly found items, or provide a kit for participants. Don't make virtual programs longer than necessary. Screen fatigue is real, so try to get your message across quickly.

Screen-time considerations. Screen time is important to consider when planning digital programs for young children. The American Academy of Pediatrics (AAP) suggests limiting screen time to no more than one hour per day for children between two and five years of age, and avoiding digital media use with children less than twenty-four months old.[2] Constructive and connective types of media, such as video chatting and interactive programs are generally exceptions to these guidelines.

Early childhood professionals are naturals at coming up with ways to make the programming engaging and constructive. Children will see and feel the energy through the screen.

"If you are doing children's programming online, I highly recommend utilizing stuffed animals," says Nicole Lawton, children's services librarian at the Naperville Public Library in Naperville, Illinois. "Kids have those on hand at home and they really engage with them. You can also have the stuffies do all of the jumping or dancing if you need a moment to catch your breath before you jump into your next activity."

There are many models in play that help guide screen-time experiences for young children. The E-Aims model, recommended by Zero to Three, encourages picking content that is engaging, meaningful, and social.

In presenting content for young children, choose content with a clear story line, engaging pictures, and interactive elements that relate to learning. You want the child to interact and engage with the content.

My best online story times have been when I actively engage with the children and see them with props from their own homes. In one program the presenter had a felt board for five green and speckled frogs. One child was wearing a frog hat, another had a prop story of five green and speckled frogs, and another brought out his plush frog collection. You would not receive this interaction during an in-person program.

Making a Plan

Every good program needs a plan. If you don't have a plan of action, you're more likely to freeze and be unprepared. Strong program preparation sets the tone for everything that comes after. An online audience can tell if you are frazzled or uncomfortable. Instructing online takes extra layers of preparation and an ability to remain calm if troubles arrive.

"Find a friend to help you get the ropes," Marcia Keyser, an online graduate support and instruction librarian at Drake University in Des Moines, Iowa, said. "And remember that everybody teaches differently. Remember that just as many students do well online as don't do so well. Make an outline of what you plan to do and fill it in the best you can."

You need to lay out scripts to use, give clear instructions in advance to minimize technical problems for your audience/students, have backup help for troubleshooting if needed, and so much more. Instructing online allows you to reach a broader audience, but it can also exclude those who are not technically savvy so you need to find ways to reach them as well.

"Prepare, prepare, prepare," said Michael Golrick, head of reference and library consultant at the State Library of Louisiana. "Do a dry run with colleagues who can critique and offer suggestions for improvement."

Access check-in. Starting a meeting with an access check-in is a best practice for accessible programming. Ask the attendees if you are speaking loud and clear enough and recommend that everyone mute their microphone to reduce background noise. Inform everyone that only one person should speak at a time, and ask if anyone needs help with digital features.

Program form, length, and timing. Determine if your program is asynchronous or synchronous, how many sessions there should be, and how long it will run. From there, work with other applicable staff to determine scheduling, timing, and duration. Remember that your regular routines or time frames may not transfer over to the virtual setting.

Be Prepared

Before the program, plan out everything you need. If you're filming, you don't want to restart several times, and if you're live, you don't want to leave a virtual room to go grab something. Make sure your computer is up-to-date, there is space available on your device for recording, and that all devices are plugged in and fully charged.

Create an agenda or script for your program and keep it close. (I tape mine on a chair, out of sight of the screen). Try to run through the aspects of your program to make sure you have everything and practice any unique concepts or new technology. I like logging on a few minutes early to make sure my audio and video work well.

Before the Program

If possible, survey your attendees before the program so you both know what to expect. If you have their email addresses, send out an introductory email or video explaining how to access the content, detailing any supplies they need to bring, and allowing participants to ask any questions. The beginning is also an ideal time to give any technology pointers to save time during the live program.

Questions to ask include: Do you need help accessing anything for this session (device, Internet, etc.)? What systems have you used before? What do you like/not like? What is the best way for you to communicate? What else should I know about you?

Advance content is helpful to prepare attendees. A technology access-and-use survey helps the presenter or technical help know everyone's comfort levels, while handouts or physical materials may get attendees excited and more invested in the program.

⊚ During the Program

1. Build anticipation with an introductory slide telling the audience what to expect (the time the program starts, any necessary supplies, an icebreaker question to type into the chat). You can even play some music to build some excitement.
2. Once you let everyone into the room, wait a few minutes so people can get their technology working. Then make any general announcements, check attendance, and list ground rules. This is also an ideal time for an access check, to make sure everyone is connected properly and can hear and see everything. Explain what to expect from the presentation as a whole.
3. Then move into the main presentation. If it's longer than an hour, try to allot time for a break at a transition period or when switching activities.
4. Take time for participation during class. Pause and give attendees time to ask questions and encourage participation through chat, hand raising, reactions, or polls. "Try to avoid just talking, or reading, for long periods of time without asking for some kind of audience participation," Chelsea Corso, children's librarian at the Barrett Paradise Friendly Library in Cresco, Pennsylvania, said.
5. Final Reflection: If appropriate, allow time for questions and reflection at the end. This time helps end class on a clear note and gives you feedback and time to make announcements about any upcoming programs or events.

"I think having a schedule and letting your viewers know what they are about to see is important," Juana Flores, children's librarian at the Kings Highway Branch for the Brooklyn Public Library in Brooklyn, New York, said. "It's okay to have hiccups and be yourself. The best program I did was not rehearsed. It didn't sound mechanical at all."

⊚ Hiring Presenters

Presenters and guest speakers are much more available in a virtual environment. Transportation fees are nonexistent and global reach is possible. A new voice makes a program more exciting for attendees and brings in unique knowledge. When scheduling presenters and events, make sure to specify that it is a virtual program and to be clear about time zones.

A way to offset costs and increase attendance is by partnering with other organizations. Everyone can share the same Zoom link and list all the sponsors.

⊚ Promotion

Promoting virtual programs is very similar to promoting in-person events. Because you can reach more people, you can spread how much you promote the event too. Discuss with your administration if you want to limit attendees to your organization's stakeholders or keep it open to everyone, and devise a plan for managing that.

Flyers, announcements, articles, social media, and word of mouth are all ways to promote programs. Share information for upcoming programs at related events and make sure all staff is aware so they can answer questions. You can make a starter copy for promotional content but tailor it depending on the medium and audience as you cross-promote programs and services via different platforms. Tailor print and digital copy for different audiences with appropriate platforms. For example, a flyer advertising a book club may have all detailed information, while a Twitter post simply has a fun tagline and the date and time.

Special audio, visual, and digital deliverables include creating a digital newsletter, a specific virtual program web page, updating the digital library and community calendars, submitting content to local TV and radio stations, or creating an electronic billboard. Reach out to community partners to promote the library's virtual programs to a different audience.

Visuals

Visual literacy is the ability to evaluate, use, and create visual media. A learner has several input and output strategies that involve decoding (taking in ideas) and encoding (creating ideas). Visuals play many roles in the learning process and may help or harm the process if not used correctly. Visuals provide a reference for ideas (icons and symbols), make abstract ideas concrete (a series of connected beads for a model of DNA), and motivate learners by getting their attention (before and after comparisons). Visual images show information differently, summarize a concept, and reduce a learning effort.

Types of visuals include pictorial symbols (a photograph or illustration), graphic symbols (a concept-related graphic or style), and verbal symbols (a verbal or written description). These symbols range from realistic to the abstract. Key ideas for visual elements and design include arrangement, balance, color, legibility, and appeal.

In digital presentations, a quality layout and sharp digital elements keep attendees engaged and give them a secondary way to process the content.

For handouts and slide shows, try to keep the layout uncluttered with white space, left-justified text, and use of headings and subheadings. Keep animations consistent and use plain language so it is reader friendly. For text, use a sans serif font that ensures access and screen readability. Avoid all-caps and large typeface and only use colors with purpose, keeping a contrast between text and background. For graphics, use visual elements consistently, and use bullets if not sequential and numbers if the list is sequential.

Academic Instruction

Online courses are most commonly offered in academic, K–12, or collegiate libraries. However, any organization can offer a recurring digital learning environment for internal training, public education, and beyond. Online courses typically combine an LMS system with some form of livestreaming or recorded videos.

I am not a school or university librarian and urge you to consult specific resources about online instruction, design, and school librarianship for detailed parameters.

Questions to ask:

- Who is my primary audience?
- Is this course required or for a grade, optional, or a pass/fail?
- What is the purpose of this course?
- How do I divide the sessions to offer quality content and information for my attendees?
- Is my course synchronous, asynchronous, or a blended learning option?

Asynchronous vs. Synchronous Courses

I've heard the comparison that synchronous learning is live TV and asynchronous is Netflix or YouTube. I say that synchronous learning is like reality TV (because people are interacting and controlling the outcome of situations).

Attendees have more control in asynchronous environments, including access to a computer, ability to move at their own pace, and ability to play a clip again. One teacher can deliver a lesson and many people can use it.

Pros of asynchronous learning include a polished product and controlled schedule by students and teachers. Cons are the feeling of teaching into the void, no real-time assessments, and less connection. Asynchronous lessons can have an expiration date by when they're locked or taken down. An "evergreen video" is content that is applicable for a long amount of time. Oftentimes how-to guides remain relevant, unless technology or hardware changes.

Setting up a strong asynchronous environment is key to a clear and welcoming digital classroom. Key elements include homepage, announcement, syllabus, faculty information, rubric, grade book, question and answer, lounge, discussion boards, lectures, Dropbox group spaces, and links to relevant resources. An idea to keep people engaged in an asynchronous environment is including time-embedded notes or quizzes in slideshows.

Many professionals, including Tina Marie Maes, lead cataloging librarian for the Madison Public Library in Madison, Wisconsin, enjoy teaching in an asynchronous environment because they can work on a flexible schedule. Maes said:

> I used Canvas to teach basic cataloging for the UW-Madison iSchool. I enjoyed the platform, ability to message the group as well as singly, and the fact that I could teach and answer questions asynchronously. I also enjoyed that it was pass/fail so grading was much easier. The setup (since I changed much of it from an early version by a different lecturer) was time-intensive but useful to make sure I knew the coursework.
>
> Make sure that you set up space in your schedule for lesson plans as well as answering students. If you are teaching asynchronously, make an option to have synchronous meetings in case students get lost. Know your material and try it out on others before presenting it.

Synchronous environments provide connections, engagement, and the ability to decipher and ask questions in real time. Downsides include the difficulty of coordinating schedules, screen fatigue, and technology issues.

Meghan Kowalski, outreach and reference librarian at the University of the District of Columbia, speaks on instructor style.

"Teaching online is different. You need to get used to the flow and how it physically feels to sit in front of a keyboard. It helps if you can find a way to get used to talking to black squares. Cameras should always be optional, which means they are almost always off. Treat this as just what is, don't fight against it, and try to be a bit performative so that you seem more lively and engaged. That allows for more connection with students even when they are just black squares."

Flipped Classroom Model

The flipped classroom model is when students engage with content first and then engage with the class and instructor. This model gives students the ability to learn at their own pace and engage one-on-one with the instructor.

"We always tried to encourage the flipped classroom model where students watched a video and then had time for Q&A. We had mixed success because most students don't watch the video," said Meghan Kowalski, outreach and reference librarian at the University of the District of Columbia. "Unless there is a small class, interactive activities don't really work because there is no in-person group peer pressure to encourage engagement."

TEXTBOX 4.3 HOMESCHOOLERS AND ONLINE LEARNING

Christina Giovanni-Caputo, librarian and educator, Chicago suburbs, Illinois:

"As a lecturer at the University of Wisconsin, Madison iSchool program, I utilize the Canvas platform to teach asynchronous lessons to MLIS students. The virtual nature of the coursework has allowed a flexible environment. I live in the Chicago area and teach remotely to Wisconsin. I teach in a virtual environment using the Moodle platform for the courses I teach through the American Library Association. I can teach asynchronous courses to at-home learners, homeschoolers, and library partnerships from my home.

"As the author of the book *Library Services to Homeschoolers: A Guide* and a customer-facing Youth Services Librarian, I urge you to learn about the at-home learners in your community. Online learning is a form of at-home learning and one of many Alternative Education Methodologies. The 2018 article 'Online Education Ascends' by Doug Lederman reported that around one-third of all enrolled college students are online learners. The national average for school-age youth according to the National Center for Education Statistics (2017) was 3.5 percent pre-COVID. And 40 percent of all homeschoolers were from marginalized communities. At the peak of the COVID-19 school closures, the United Nations Educational, Scientific and Cultural Organization (https://en.unesco.

org/) recorded that 90 percent of all youth globally were learning from home. The US Census Household Pulse Survey showed in May 2021 at-home learning was at around 20 percent. There are various reasons behind families' choices to school from home. Specific to online learning, some states have K–12 virtual school (for example Florida Virtual School) options and families may have enjoyed the flexibility that remote schooling can bring. There are families that travel in recreational vehicles, that have shared their gratitude with me on toy circulation. Another family unenrolled their trans child from school during the transition, and the child is schooling online. There is a growing number of MLIS students working toward their degrees online. The online subscription-based K–12 curricula that is available to families is vast and deep, with many diverse options. I recommend surveying the Alternative Educational community surrounding each library, as each community will have a different need. How each family schools and/or unschools is personal, and the public library can support them on their educational journey.

"Please join the conversation with other librarians as we navigate how to foster belonging and serve homeschoolers on Facebook (www.facebook.com/groups/1616005898516578/)."

Aspects of Online Courses

Types of students include elementary and family learners, at-risk students with special needs, high schoolers, college and graduate students, adult learners, and continuing education learners.

Syllabus. A strong syllabus should have all relevant class information including a course outline, general expectations, office hours, grading policies, and information to request accommodations.

Sample class outline. An online course is very similar to an in-person program. Opening procedures include attendance, a welcome, an access chat, and any ground rules. Then, the main portion of the program begins, followed by a review, goodbyes, and casual time for people to stick around for questions.

Design considerations. Factors to consider when looking at a course's design include the ability to quickly locate materials, clearly communicated instructor hours, easy access to the syllabus, course technology requirements, technical support options and troubleshooting, accessibility information, and course functionality.

Attendance. See if your organization has an official attendance policy that covers how much of the class needs to attend and how they prove their presence. "I take attendance in my class and sometimes students will log in but then leave," said Melody Friedenthal, public services librarian at the Worcester Public Library in Worcester, Massachusetts. "I ask all students to turn on their cameras, if their computer has one. I make sure I ask questions to every student, whether or not I can see their face. If they don't respond, I mark them absent (students must attend all six sessions in order to get a Certificate of Completion)."

Common mistakes: General mistakes made in an online class include skipping class, missing an assignment, losing email, asking redundant questions, not following instructions, not submitting on time, or only participating once a week. A policy should address what happens in the above situations.

Distractions: Common distractions in an online classroom include students using a second device, off-screen "multi-tasking," and side conversations. Updating settings in advanced features and using a general code of conduct can help reduce distractions.

TEXTBOX 4.4

Spotlight on Amanda Jones, SLJ's 2021 School Librarian of the Year and teacher-librarian at Live Oak Middle School in Denham Springs, Los Angeles.

"I am most proud of my Journey with Jones virtual field trips. I host them live and also record them for teachers to use in their classrooms. We did fun trips, but also trips in collaboration with their teachers'/subject standards. I have partnered with other schools and the public library on several trips.

"My biggest challenge was that I knew absolutely nothing about online instruction. Very quickly, I listened to my PLN, watched webinars, and learned platforms on my own so that I could keep our school library program going while we were virtual.

"I think my favorite Journey with Jones virtual trip was the Mars Perseverance trip. We had over fifty students attend the live session and it was just something we did for fun the week before the rover landing. I really got into acting like I was at Mission Control, and NASA has some wonderful videos and resources that were available to view. I think it was my favorite trip for these reasons, and also because it was on something current that the students were excited to learn about that was happening in space.

"School librarians really stepped up to the plate during virtual instruction. School librarians stepped up to the plate by posting resources, tutorials, how-to guides, utilizing online platforms, and creating and sharing content (like webinars) for all stakeholders—students, teachers, parents, and the community. Everywhere you looked there was information from school librarians online for just about any topic you needed help with to continue programming in a virtual environment. School librarians proved that they were school leaders and showed how powerful a school librarian can be for a school."

Engaging Content

Chapters 3 and 5 provide information about engaging sessions and gaining participant buy-in. Chapter 8 outlines specific digital resources that are helpful in online learning.
Other ideas for engaging content in academic settings are:

- Targeted and active class discussion, both synchronous and asynchronous
- Social media and discussion forums (community based, question and answer, weekly topics)
- Guided journal or blog writing with individual and teacher reflections
- Classroom shared knowledge base with a collaborative glossary or annotated bibliography (wiki, Google, or Facebook Groups)

- Practice exercises and self-assessments (multiple choice, fill in the blank, gap-fill, drag and drop, matching, true and false questions)
- Group project presentations and research projects
- Digital meeting room may vary for various learners (group for sharing, individual work, and for teacher assignments)
- Providing a choice board and multiple options for an assignment speaks to different learners and is helpful for those with accessibility issues. For example, one can choose to either draw a photo, create a wiki, or edit a video.
- Activities and tools
- Use different meeting rooms for different learners, for example: one group for sharing, one for teacher help, and another for individual work

It is ideal to transform materials into activities, try to change presenters, incorporate varied media, and use a mixed setup. Breaking up content into the appropriate subject matter makes it easier to navigate and understand. Try referencing resources from different sources (library, the Internet, databases, interviews, etc.) and to provide frequent opportunities for self-reflection. Students are busy, and if you show them that time has value and make learning personal, engagement will ideally increase.

"Hook students right away," said Stephanie Dietrich, learning commons director for District 203 in Naperville, Illinois. "I always start my sessions with a quick online poll, which is usually just a ridiculous trivia question. The kids love it and it sets the tone that we are going to have a fun interactive session."

Means of Participation

There are several options to include students in participation. Breakout rooms help students go into small groups, but they may need a procedure. Volunteering requires hand raising, while using chat is optional and everyone can do it. *Cold call* is when the teacher simply calls on someone. *Speed question* is seeing who answers first, and *wait question* is a pause before answering.

In classrooms especially, depending on the students' age range, parent and guardian information is key.

"It's hard to keep students interested online," Dietrich said. "Make sure you include interactive activities and keep lecturing to a minimum. Use breakout rooms for students to interact with each other and keep things interesting."

Cheating. There are more opportunities for cheating in the digital environment. Remote proctoring is an idea to stop cheating. Requiring students to turn on their camera or microphone for at least a minute is a way to make sure the proper person is present. Assessments can stay live for a predetermined time limit or require completion from a specific location.

Plagiarism is an issue in all forms of writing. Instructors can teach what plagiarism is, explain how web copying is plagiarism and cite online search engines. Many online plagiarism checkers exist, along with LMS systems for monitoring student activity. Apps for plagiarism include Turnitin, SafeAssign, and Plagiarism Detector.

Assessment

Assessment methods vary depending on the student. Types of assessment can help in a classroom:

Cold call: The act of calling on students who have not raised their hand.

Show call: Take written work and display on screen.

Implicit assessment: Students check their own work against a model (but might not do it).

Lagging assessment: Submit for later grading.

Real-time assessment: Answering in the moment (which can slow down pacing).

Ideas for assessments include reflections and portfolios.

Chromebooks

Many educational institutions offer Chromebooks for students. They work well with Google products and are easy to use but have differences from the standard computer. Chromebooks are small with a longer battery life, are cost effective, and have a smaller operating system. Google Drive works offline.

Chromebook quick tips:

- To use a Chromebook, you need a Google account.
- The power button is in a unique location, top right corner.
- Delete button is Alt + backspace.
- Top row has options to switch pages in browser history, open in full-page view, reload page, switch to next window, brightness, sound, and power buttons.
- The trackpad is more sensitive than a click trackpad. It only needs a slight finger tap to draw an object. For right click, press or tap with two fingers. To scroll, move two fingers up or down depending on which direction you want to go. To scroll between web pages, use two fingers with one straight stroke across.
- Swipe across with three fingers to move between tabs.

Best Practices

Practice, practice, practice. If you want to use a new tool, test it out first. If you've never created a course before, make a sample one. If you're worried about connectivity, do a test run. You cannot stop all technical problems from happening, but you can decrease the likelihood.

Be present at the course site. It is important that the instructor is present. This presence may include active involvement in chat forums, arriving early and staying late at live meetings, and actively checking all modes of communication.

Create boundaries. Going off of the above tip, it is important to create boundaries and make it known that you are *not* available 24/7. Digital office hours and posted times stating work hours can establish boundaries. As outlined in chapter 2, presence can differ between social, teaching, and cognitive presences.

Incorporate active learning. Especially in a digital environment, active learning keeps people from losing focus and breaks up the class.

"You can do it," said Julia Frederick, early literacy librarian at the Vernon Area Public Library in Lincolnshire, Illinois. "It can feel super daunting knowing how to interact with folks, but don't think too hard about it. Do what you would do in person, but try to adapt it. For example, oftentimes in story time, we'll count to five on our fingers and then I'll ask everyone to give me a high five through their screen (I hold my hand up to the camera and show them my palm and ask them to give me or their grown-up a high five). Almost everyone tried to high-five me."

Collaborative learning is beneficial. Group projects play an even bigger role in digital learning because it is one of the few times attendees can get to know other participants. The value of learning from others' experiences and listening to their input is sometimes more valuable than premade course content.

Provide information in multiple mediums. There are a variety of learners who all process information in different ways. Having multiple mediums to access information helps reach a larger number of learners.

Adapt as you go. One of the best pieces of advice I've received is to "always have a plan, but then be ready to change that plan." You realize that none of the attendees are following you. Or you may find that the organic conversation leads you into a different topic that is still relevant. Or you may find that the technology you thought would be perfect simply fails. It is important to have a backup plan, to watch your attendees for cues, and to be ready to change course as needed.

Avoid common pitfalls. Teaching pitfalls are easy to fall into, especially in an online environment when it is harder to read the audience. Try to guide in your guidance and not simply instruct or lecture, and to practice active listening, allowing wait time for people to either type in the chat, raise their hand, or ask a question.

Stay authentic. Attendees can tell if you are nervous or reading from a script. Maintain your natural teaching presence.

Stay concise and clear. It is easy for tone to get lost in a virtual world. Read your text over before sending, and keep it on-point.

Consistency. Running sessions in a similar format helps learners gain comfort and familiarity.

Intention. There is a vast pool of options to choose from for online learning. Think about what activities you choose and why.

Speak slowly and clearly. The web makes it harder for people to hear so remember to check for understanding and find moments to pause for questions.

Look at the screen. A fun tip is to put googly eyes where the camera is or an arrow by the webcam to remember where to look.

Self-Reflection

When planning programming, take time to think about what you have done, how far you have come, and what you can accomplish in the future. So often, we go into overdrive and *do, do, do* without taking time to stop and reflect. Breathing and thinking about what you and your organization needs saves time in the long run.

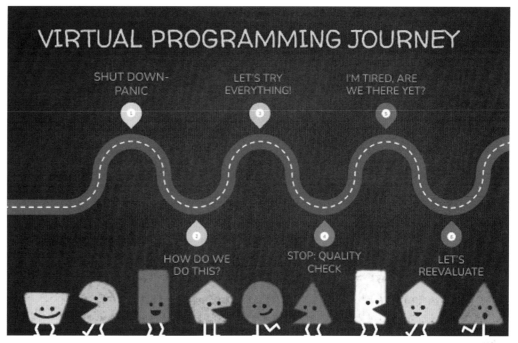

Figure 4.2. COVID-19 virtual programming road map. *Emily Mroczek, Slide Carnival*

Self-reflection questions include: What did I have planned in "the before"? Is there anything I tried early in the pandemic worth trying again? What is *not* working? What are we capable of doing? What does our population want and need? What is our new normal?

Key Points

- Don't be afraid to make changes. Digital learning is a flexible and fluid environment that is constantly evolving.
- Digital programs require most of the same preparation and concepts as in-person programs with additional measures for accessibility, technology, and interaction.
- Weigh your options on the type of program depending on the audience, purpose, and scope of the program.

Further Reading

Ostman, Sarah. *Going Virtual: Programs and Insights from a Time of Crisis.* Chicago: ALA Editions, 2021.

"Virtual Storytime Services Guide." Association for Library Service to Children (ALSC), February 26, 2021. www.ala.org/alsc/virtual-storytime-services-resource-guide.

⊚ Notes

1. "Leep Online," School of Information Sciences, accessed November 1, 2021, https://ischool.illinois.edu/degrees-programs/ms-library-and-information-science/mslis-leep-online.

2. "Media and Children," American Academy of Pediatrics, accessed September 2, 2021, www.aap.org/en/patient-care/media-and-children/.

Building Community

WHEN DISCUSSING ONLINE LEARNING, one issue that constantly comes up is lack of community and connection. People think it's impossible to create the same connections on the Internet as in real life. As someone who has hundreds of "pocket friends," from Facebook, Twitter, and now Zoom, I beg to differ. As technology evolves, digital media is a tool for social connection that allows for more interaction than ever before. As shown during the COVID-19 pandemic, people can connect and socialize without being physically together.

"The world has become a much closer society," Melanie Taylor Coombs, the adult services supervisor and librarian at the McArthur Library in Biddeford, Maine, said. "We welcomed people from all around the world with our online experiences. That is the beautiful part of an online environment. Best advice: Do not be afraid to try anything."

In this chapter, we look at using technology as a tool for connection, interaction, and friendship. The content in this chapter is simply ideas. Determining your style and presence is up to you. Think about yourself and your organization's mission and purpose.

Creating a Positive Atmosphere

Atmosphere is one of the most difficult things to control, yet it's an important aspect of both online and in-person environments. People are not going to engage and participate if they don't feel welcome, comfortable, and safe. Ideas to create this atmosphere include having clear and concise communication, being flexible and understanding, and doing your best to build a community. Remember that no community is perfect and that some sessions are going to run better than others. Just like with pedagogy, try to create the culture you are hoping for and let the technology supplement that culture.

The growth mindset often transfers easily to digital formats and ensuring to convey effort and intention for the community, along with cultural expectations. Try to adapt your course to the attendees, influence online conversations, advance multimedia with personalization, foster collaborative learning, and support intelligent communication. Characteristics of a positively infused classroom include information-rich, differentiated resources for multiple learning styles, connected and personalized. There are so many qualities of a strong online instructor, as illustrated in the word cloud in figure 5.1.

Figure 5.1. Word cloud: qualities of a dynamic online instructor. *Emily Mroczek, Free Word Cloud Generator*

These characteristics may seem impossible to achieve, but the more you practice the more you will see what methods work in online instruction, just like a seasoned in-person instructor. Try asking your attendees what characteristics are most important to them, then prioritize what you want to achieve and come up with concrete ways of achieving your coveted characteristics.

Attendees are more likely to engage if their contributions and opinions have weight. Public encouragement helps motivate and keep everyone on track. Ideas for creating a positive environment and building community include:

Surveys at the beginning, middle, and end of a session where attendees indicate anything they are hoping to learn about.

Round-robin check-ins where attendees can take turns talking and saying hello, put an answer in the chat, or respond with an emoji. Remember that everyone has diverse talents and individuals may work better if they have options for how to respond, learn, and work.

Choice boards are graphic organizers that allow attendees different ways to learn about a particular concept. There are templates for choice boards on various applications. The most common ideas are Bingo or Tic Tac Toe, where people can choose activities to complete.

Polling is an interactive way to receive fast responses. Chapter 8 outlines several poll tools where you ask students questions and the poll shows responses. If used correctly, polls are a powerful supplement to discussions.

Talk to your attendees. If you know who your attendees are, they may have opinions about program formats and be more likely to share outside of the session. Reaching out to potential participants helps keep satisfaction and participation high.

Heidi Fowler, a reference librarian for the Grafton Public Library in Grafton, Massachusetts, said flexibility is important and can help you decide what program to use. "If you have time, figure out in advance what your regulars (at the very least) like for online interactions," Fowler said. "I have one very regular participant who does not like to type. She's self-conscious about typos and spelling mistakes and doesn't think she is quick enough to keep up with the conversation."

Leave time for reflection. If you want people to respond to or think about something, they need time to do so. Say something like "I'd like you to think about . . . ," and take a short pause. Then, either say your own response or solicit answers from the students. The silence may feel awkward, but it is okay. You can post responses and questions later if you don't have time to get to anything. Then, your attendees will still feel valued for responding.

Guest speakers. Guest speakers amplify the room and promote engagement, diversity, and inclusion. It switches up the atmosphere hearing from someone different and brings in varying perspectives.

Expand the community. Try developing ways people can meet behind-the-scenes staff members like administration, technical assistants, or content creators. Ideas include behind-the-scenes videos, photographs, backstage tours, or guest speakers.

Have fun. The instructor guides the environment. Encourage people to take time for mental health and self-care. Make appropriate comments about what is on people's screens, celebrate birthdays and special events, and narrate the positive that is happening.

Train the trainer. Allow attendees to train the trainer, give suggestions, and talk about the best digital session they ever attended. Attendees could even plan or lead a part of a session if appropriate.

Read the room. Look around and see what works best for you and your attendees. Does talking in chat or speaking verbally work better?

The digital format allows for many ways to create a unique and collaborative learning community. Students could vote on a class, name, image, or slogan.

There are many strategies to build an effective digital learning community as outlined by Rena M. Palloff and Keith Pratt.[1] Key strategies include: clearly defining the purpose of the group, defining norms and a clear code of conduct, allowing for a range of member roles, allowing for and facilitating subgroups, and allowing members to resolve their own disputes.

A general standard where everyone shows their face through a webcam can promote community. Think about asking students to turn on video as a key part of participation. Keep in mind that students may feel uncomfortable sharing their personal circumstances and video cannot be required because of privacy concerns. Remind your students about the option for virtual backgrounds and encourage them to post a fun photo if they are not comfortable with their camera on. I also like to remind people they can turn their cameras off and on.

Having designated people in different roles can help create a calm vibe and community feel. As mentioned in chapter 3, typical roles include a chat monitor, co-teacher, and technology support while more unique roles are a designated skeptic who acts as the voice of dissent, and a studio audience member who makes "obvious" reactions.

General group interaction transfers easily into the digital format. Decide what works best for the activity at hand. Breakout groups often work better in the digital format because they are a way to separate people and build connections, and you don't need to organize a physical space for multiple groups. Groups can work together using breakout rooms, chat channels, or collaborative tools like Google Docs. You can group people randomly or based on shared experiences and interests (homogenous groups) or make a balance of different skills (heterogeneous groups). Group participants can split themselves into roles that work best for them: leader, editor, submitter, and so on.

Additional ideas for building community:

- Post pictures of students on the course website.
- Request fun facts from attendees and put them in a slideshow or use them to create a "getting to know you" discussion.
- Document activities from live courses and post on the course website.
- Encourage biographies, profiles, and personal interaction.
- Put short surveys on the website and then exhibit the results on the web.

ⓖ Instructor-Attendee Relationships

A positive relationship with the instructor improves the overall class experience. Make an effort to greet people individually, offer yourself for one-on-one video chats, and use chat in different ways. For example, encourage asking individual questions via their private chat, chatting with the instructor individually, and then have the instructor read it aloud. One-on-one video chats with the instructor can also be a way to bond. These chats don't have to be formal—speaking before or after class works too.

Participant commitment increases if the instructor shows passion and commitment.

Try to personalize the online experience for students by asking them to suggest online tools, rules, and guidelines for the overall flow of the class. I like to ask what people are expecting to learn that day or in general, so then I can tailor content to their individual needs.

The easiest way to do this is to lead by example. If you greet participants and write answers with positivity and engagement, others are more likely to do the same. Ask the attendees for possible next steps and responses.

As an instructor of digital learners, the pressure can be monumental. Not only do the usual expectations of helping participants learn and enjoy themselves hold, but there's also the pressure of making sure that technology runs smoothly and doesn't hinder the learning experience. It's important to remember that nothing is ever going to be perfect and you cannot please everyone. Do your best to make sure you are reaching as many learners as possible, but remember we are all human.

Establish positive relationships by ensuring participants have access and familiarity with technology, establishing guidelines and procedures, and being a model for participation, collaboration, and reflection. For an instructor, taking a session to the next level may not be upping the content but changing the presentation or interactivity to reach participants. It is helpful to think of various motivators and multiple opportunities for success, not so different from a traditional learning environment.

It is beneficial in an online environment if the role of teachers shifts more to a coach style of guiding and mentoring. This relationship can help students connect in the digital world. Online learning asks students to be more active and conduct their personal learning experiences, but that might prove more difficult for many learners, especially those who have never engaged in online education before. It can help to do an informal survey at the start of class to gauge participant's prior knowledge of the course content and technology in general.

Especially when using technology, I always prefer the group effort approach. If someone has a problem, I might direct them to another participant that I saw working on something similar. I always tell other instructors that "You don't need to have all the answers. Just help people find the answers."

Also, try to be aware of your attendees' differences with technology, meet them where they are, and provide different options. Think about your language and communication style.

⊚ Partnerships

Partnering with other libraries or organizations in the community can decrease the workload and help attendees create a bigger sense of community. It also helps build connections for your attendees and adds unique perspectives. I've seen libraries or schools come together to host large events, and accomplish a higher level of success by combining resources.

Potential partnerships include local park districts, schools and universities, painting or cooking organizations that would like to do a demonstration (any local business owners), museums, and nonprofit organizations.

"Managing big crowds and various ages and skill levels is a challenge," said Paul Addis, reference librarian at the Coos Bay Public Library in Coos Bay, Oregon. "I am handling this by partnering more with other organizations and individuals, and using volunteers and co-workers to help me with Zoom sessions. Being able to engage my community with folks around the world has been really awesome. I have a deaf man from Armenia who attends my ASL program and it's so cool to see him and folks from Canada engaging with locals from our community."

⊚ Fun Activities

The digital environment provides a plethora of opportunities for digital games and experiences that can break up a session and make it more engaging.

There are easy icebreakers that move from one student to another, or more intensive role playing where two students could act something out as if in the physical classroom. A whiteboard or Jamboard is a fun way to play Would You Rather? Simple energizers help break things up, like brain teasers, chair yoga, guessing a photo, and showing what's outside your window. Another fun way of sharing in Zoom or asynchronous interactions is showing pets or babies.

Other games that work well in the digital environment are providing a sentence starter and having attendees complete the sentence in a chat, asking an experience question and having attendees change a status to show their response, or playing a "guess the song" game. Another idea is where everyone draws a sixty-second sketch and shares their results.

"Polls are great, and Jamboards are fun, particularly if you get to use GIFs," said Meghan Kowalski, outreach and reference librarian at the University of the District of Columbia. "But keep this short or students will melt away. Ask to see pets. That is always a great way to bring some levity and engagement."

Time before a session starts or during breaks is ideal to build energy. You can play videos or welcome music and have people vote on or suggest what to play to make it more fun. Or put up a slide with an icebreaker asking people to introduce themselves, solve a riddle, or share something fun about where they are taking the online course from.

Beyond the Instructor

A truly connected and community-centered class has relationships beyond the instructor. Facilitating partner and group work, ideas for volunteering and internships, and guest lecturers are ways to help people increase their comfort with others.

Contact theory is a hypothesis in psychology that states prejudice and conflict between groups reduces if the groups interact with one another. Try to find ways for attendees to get to know one another beyond the typical classroom. The easiest way to do this is for introductory discussion posts and profiles that include everyone's name, location, professional background, and personal information. Video introductions are also a fun way to discover someone's personality. Always sign your name when posting and don't make assumptions or stereotypes about others. Wait for attendees to provide the information they are comfortable with.

Encourage attendees to celebrate their successes with one another. Don't hesitate to connect people with one another.

Not all discussions need to be synchronous. You can decide if topic-driven or social-driven discussions will benefit your attendees more and find meaningful prompts for them to connect over. Topic-driven discussions help to highlight specific content, while social-driven discussions connect more with current events. There's also the idea of the discussion board as a digital water cooler, which can help people engage and have fun with one another.

Attendees could create a social-networking forum to continue collection, plan aspects of the class like a themed or costume day, and even plan a socially distanced meet-up.

Key Points

- Find activities that work best for yourself and your attendees.
- Prioritize the attitude and behaviors that would best benefit yourself and your attendees.
- Provide attendees a sense of ownership and belonging in your sessions.

⊚ Further Reading

Finkelstein, Jonathan. *Learning in Real Time: Synchronous Teaching and Learning Online.* San Francisco: Jossey-Bass, A John Wiley & Sons Imprint, 2006.

⊚ Note

1. Rena M. Palloff and Keith L. Pratt, *Building Online Learning Communities: Effective Strategies for the Virtual Classroom* (San Francisco: Jossey-Bass Publishers, 2007).

Choosing a Platform

THE DIGITAL PLATFORM IS THE HEART of the physical components of online instruction. However, the selection of tools should come after you understand your presentation and what you want to help develop it. You may have the authority to decide what platform you use, however, for the vast majority of organizations, administration makes platform-specific decisions. Information about the various platforms is helpful if you want to make a point for switching or trying something new for a specific program.

It's understandable and workable for an organization to use multiple platforms, depending on the specific audience and purpose. The platform can change based on factors including the program's goals, attendees' needs, and technological desires. Consider your own technology skills when deciding how to present content. It is best to use media you are familiar with or have easy access to technology support for. Also, an institution may have a preexisting contract with a specific medium and you have no choice. Most platforms have videos, tutorials, and online networks, which are helpful to conquer the learning curve.

Choosing a Platform

Platforms feature varying capabilities for screen sharing, commenting, and more. The same platform that works well for a public virtual story-time performance may not work well for facilitating virtual book clubs, hosting a meeting, or teaching a course.

Think about the number of people likely to access your content and how to ensure everyone in the community can enjoy your virtual programs and services. In general, free versions of programs have limited features and premiums allow more customization and time. Typically, the host needs to purchase a premium account, and attendees can benefit from the perks.

Questions to ask when choosing a platform include:

- Who is using this technology and what are their capabilities (both instructors and students)?
- What types of communication do you want to have (email, chat, whiteboard, audio, video, asynchronous, synchronous)?
- Are assessments necessary and what types of assessment and grading do you want?
- Are you looking for feedback or statistics?
- What accessibility features do you need?
- When and how often do upgrades take place?
- What is the budget? Keep the number of licenses and discounts in mind.
- What server, client, device, and network requirements exist for the tool to run effectively?
- What features would be most helpful (time constraints, participant constraints, level of interactivity, chat functions)?
- What technical support is available for these options (from both the platform and your individual organization)?
- Is the interface easy to understand and user-friendly?
- How much training does this interface require?
- How well does this media integrate with other platforms?
- How much time do you expect participants to be learning collaboratively and synchronously versus individually and asynchronously?

All the above questions can help determine your top priorities when deciding on a new platform, which include accessibility, interactivity, compatibility, and budget. Making a priority list of your top features, or categorizing features into need, want, and desire, is a helpful way to narrow down your priorities.

This chapter provides an overview of the various platforms and their key features to determine which platform meets your needs. Please note platform options are constantly changing. Consult the service provider for up-to-date information, pricing, and features.

Learning Management Systems

Learning management systems (LMS), are the central hubs for online learning. This hub is where participants can find the syllabus, submit assignments, post in discussion forums, and more. Commonly used in classes as the central hub or a mission control center, an LMS also works for a book club, project team, or other group that has ongoing and asynchronous conversations. These help to streamline conversations and information.

Blackboard

Blackboard provides collaboration and a user-friendly management system. The company aims to integrate technology and address individual educational needs. The wide range of products support people from kindergarten to higher and further education to the workplace and government. There are many different systems depending on the organization and needs, including Blackboard Learn, Blackboard for Education, and Blackboard for Business. Various packages can be pricey, and an organization needs to commit.

Pros: Strong import tools, course hosting, and moderate to complex usages.

Cons: Help requests can prove difficult as they must go through local hubs first. Blackboard is not the most compatible with various systems. It has not kept up with other LMSes regarding ease of use.

Accessibility: Pairs well with screen readers; has designated landmarks based on Accessible Rich Internet Applications (ARIA) Suite; allows for keyboard navigation and shortcuts, customizable content pages, interactive tools, content editor math formulas, and links to Blackboard Alexa.[1]

Tips and tricks: Customize courses to individual needs by hiding and showing columns and moving items around. Make use of embedding and mashing up content with outside sources.

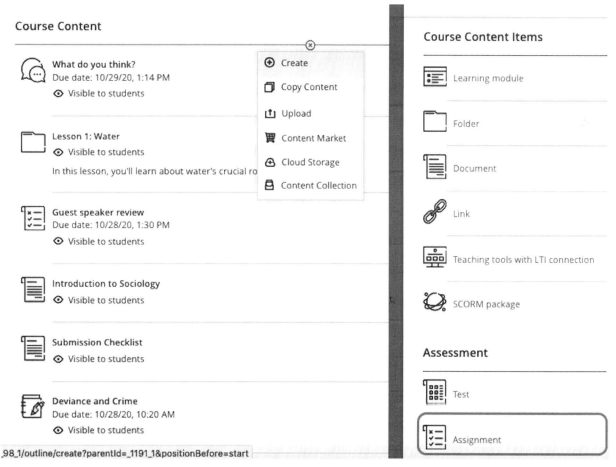

Figure 6.1. Blackboard instructor dashboard. *Blackboard*

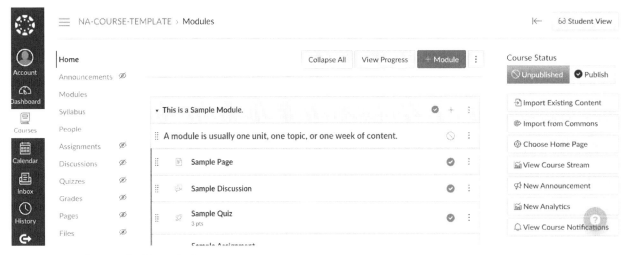

Figure 6.2. Canvas dashboard. *Canvas*

Canvas

A high-speed and sleek-looking learning system that serves as a collaborative workspace. K–12 schools, colleges, and businesses use Canvas. The LMS features integrations with various apps and connections with a strong educator community. The six focuses are learning management, assessment, content, online programs, analytics, and professional development. Teacher accounts are free with various options and plans ranging in cost.[2]

Pros: Multiple discussion options, a secure messaging system, strong customer support, and clear instructions. Instructors receive creativity options for their virtual spaces, and there are many different viewing options. Users personalize pages, collaborate on documents, share lessons, and use the Canvas Commons.

Cons: A large beginning learning curve, especially for new users. Customization is difficult, and limited chat capabilities and hard-to-use grading features exist. Not the most intuitive and there can be discussion board issues and high cost.

Tips and tricks: Take time to explore the different options and views so you can tell what people are looking at. Also, take time to explore unique features including modules, question banks, templates, timestamps, and "blueprint" master copies.

Accessibility features: Canvas is compatible with many screen reader softwares, has movable components so users can create a screen that meets their needs, and has keyboard shortcuts. Special accessibility features include audio notifications for the chat tool, customizable font settings, a rich content editor, and special user settings with high contrast UI and underline links.

Google Classroom

This central hub based off of Google provides a home base of Google interfaces for anyone with a Google account.[3] While it's a strong support system with many resources, it is exclusive to Google products through Google for Education including Gmail, Google Calendar, Google Drive, Google Docs, Google Sites, YouTube, and Google Classroom.

This LMS can be ideal for authoring individual documents, sharing, and editing. An instructor creates a class in Google Classroom, provides attendees with an invite code, and begins sharing documents, information, and communications. Google Classroom

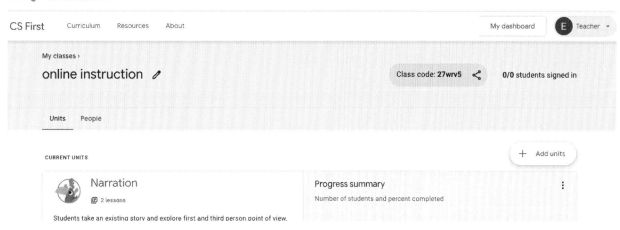

Figure 6.3. Google Classroom teacher dashboard. *Google Classroom*

integrates with the Google workspace environment and provides live videos using Google Meet. The primary interface is free, with paid options for teaching, learning, and education, which offer plagiarism checks, more cloud storage, and malware detection.

Pros: Ideal for organizations with small budgets, centralizes Google tools, and is very user-friendly for people of all ages and skill sets. Free, intuitive, and can post to an individual or all student accounts.

Cons: Google Classroom has limited features, and your content is not for long-term use. Reusing materials for future sessions is difficult. Some of the intricate classroom differences, for example, materials and assignments, can be difficult to grasp. Student accounts have a lot of control. Grade book integration can be complicated.

Accessibility features: Large amounts of Chrome extensions provide magnification, voice typing, and braille support. Keyboard shortcuts can save time navigating the system.

Tips and tricks: Use various comment types depending on your purpose: class comments, private comments, and comments in a file. You can add multiple attachments to one assignment, which can be helpful for a variety of templates or examples. You can view the history on a classroom and see which users have made changes and edits.

The #GoogleClassroom community is huge, so don't hesitate to reach out on social media and find a network of support. There is a free app for Classroom, which allows sharing on other Google apps. Many organizations may block YouTube, and Google has a workaround. You can attach videos to the playlist stored in Google Drive, and attendees can access the video right in Google Classroom without having to navigate to multiple websites. Additional fun features are observing other classrooms, syncing with school directories, and creating an Ad Hoc Playlist.

Moodle

Moodle is a modular open sourced system based on plug ins to develop and manage courses online.[4] It has a customizable layout and a large user base but lacks more recent updates. It's a commonly used learning management platform that many people may have experience with. Moodle supports teaching and learning worldwide, with extensive documentation and resources available. There are options for teaching and workplaces.

Figure 6.4. Moodle instructor dashboard. *Moodle*

Pros: The open-source approach means Moodle is constantly up-to-date. Moodle is available in about 120 languages and is compatible with most devices. Moodle supports asynchronous learning and is easy to install.

Cons: There are a limited number of plug-ins. Although easy to install, it can be hard to configure with other plug-ins.

Accessibility: Moodle's goal is accessibility for all users regardless of their ability. It has a voluntary product accessibility template and a running list of prioritized accessibility concerns that is kept up-to-date and updated.

Tips and tricks: Clean up your site with colors, designs, and hiding unnecessary information. Glossary blocks and labels can pull in learners, and you can embed RSS and Twitter feeds to share relevant information.

Schoology

A school-based system that has many options for assignments and assessments, Schoology integrates learning management, assessment, and professional development. It allows for visual insights into student performance and offers integration of classroom tools, productivity tools, and individual apps.[5] There are free and enterprise versions, including

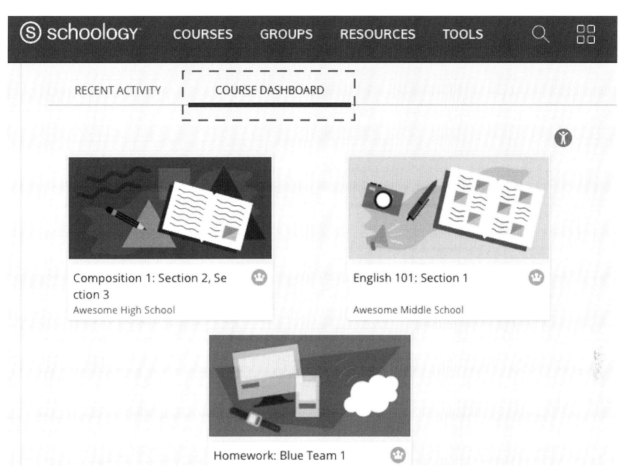

Figure 6.5. Schoology dashboard. *Schoology*

a one-time licensing fee with pricing dependent on the number of students. Schoology is be a strong resource with places that use a lot of Google products but opt out of Google Classroom.

Pros: Auto rostering, parent and guardian access, allows for organization in different instructional models. Connectivity with Google products is helpful for users. In discussion boards you can see how often someone has participated. There are built-in assessment tools and a plagiarism checker, and you can save questions for the future.

Cons: The assessments can prove complicated with varying learners, and Schoology does not transfer well onto various devices. It can be hard to navigate various pages and it is hard to preview. It can be costly and not always the most reliable. The designs are outdated and not intuitive.

Accessibility: Schoology has a Voluntary Accessibility Template that explains how it works to support content.

Tips and tricks: Color-coding helps organization, along with special tools such as add assessment, rubrics, and page features.

Additional learning management systems include: Seesaw (ideal for younger classrooms to promote student engagement), Thinkific (highlights multimedia content and offers courses in thematic bundles), Edmodo (education software that boasts compatibility with Common Core standards), Eduflow (helpful for corporate training and higher education with free and paid versions), Chamilo (open-source flexibility with free sign-up but paid courses), D2L Brightspace (game-based and video-friendly learning advertised toward the K–12 audience), and iSpring (ideal for training projects with offline and online options along with webinar capability).

⌬ Videoconferencing Services

Videoconferencing is most commonly used for online instruction. The ability to see and hear instructors and other participants is the easiest way to mimic an in-person experience. Web conferencing tools usually enable attendees to share their screen, audio, video, and messages. The magnitude of events held over videoconferencing platforms is awe-inspiring.

Live presentations allow for real-time interaction between the provider and library patrons at home. Feedback and questions are instant. Many of the programs include marketing tools, technical support, and landing pages. There are many different videoconferencing systems out there, with new ones getting added (or phased out), but here is a snapshot of a few of the popular ones at the time of publication. Many of these services can integrate with LMS platforms, and the introductory questions can apply when deciding on the best platform for you.

Livestreaming refers to content that your patrons access in real time. Patrons can view content and interact with the presenter as it is happening, generally via mobile or digital recording devices. These programs have a more authentic feeling, as they happen in the moment. There is generally less opportunity for staff to polish or edit the final product beyond any practice they may have in advance of filming. While most of these programs happen in real time, there are also workarounds that hosts can use to livestream and pre-record videos as well.

Adobe Connect

Adobe Connect is a software suite with remote training, presentation, and desktop sharing. Meeting rooms divide into "pods," with different functions. Adobe Connect advertises as a virtual stage for telling stories. Meeting plans allow different numbers of hosts and participants, but the free version only allows for three participants.

Pros: An appealing interface, organized pods, strong connections, and customization.

Cons: Limited ability to monitor events. Internet connection needed for all editing can prove cumbersome. It is a costly option that often requires extensive technical support.

Accessibility: Extensive keyboard functions, options for changing bandwidths, tab navigation, closed captioning, and color customization.

Tips and tricks: To reduce bandwidth, pause your webcam, use call-in options, and edit the screen quality in preferences.

From the field: "Adobe Connect is great for presentations, breakout rooms, polls, and sharing screens. I have been using it for six or seven years," said Michael Golrick, head of reference and library consultant for the State Library of Louisiana. "Discussions are harder in Adobe Connect than in some other platforms (Zoom), and the way we use it, we do not see the students/participants—that can be a shortcoming. There is no visual feedback from those in the session."

Blackboard Collaborate

Blackboard Collaborate is a videoconferencing tool that allows file and application sharing along with a virtual whiteboard. Blackboard Collaborate offers plans with various privileges and capabilities.

Pros: Extensive features include breakout rooms, live polling, live captions, and chat.

Cons: Many similarities to Zoom but less ease of access to the public. Requires a high bandwidth, and the more attendees, the more difficult connectivity is. Features including the timer and chat typing indicator discontinued when usage picked up during COVID-19.

Accessibility: Offers a Voluntary Product Accessibility Template, available in English. Screen reader browser support, keyboard navigation, functional test support.

Tips and tricks: Designate someone to monitor the chat. In the event of a delayed login, retry multiple times. Test sharing any files, and use the recommended web browsers (Chrome or Firefox).

From the field: Marcia Keyser, an online graduate support and instruction librarian at Drake University in Des Moines, Iowa, said, "My university uses Blackboard Ultra. I like that I can put each meeting of the class into a section."

BlueJeans

A Verizon company with cloud-based videoconferencing, BlueJeans hosts online meetings, webinars, and video calls. The latest plans include unlimited recordings and real-time transcription. Options including BlueJeans Rooms, Meetings, Gateway, Telehealth, and Events can change to fit an organization's needs. BlueJeans boasts its real-time intelligence, easy access, and high security. A variety of service plans are available with annual and monthly options.

Pros: Integrates well with Microsoft Teams, strong online support, and user-friendly control console. Consistent reviews of high quality and speed.

Cons: Many permissions stay with a single moderator, including loading video and controlling slides.

Accessibility: Automated closed captioning for desktop users, hot keys and shortcuts, participant pinning, ability to add accessibility options in profile.

Tips and tricks: Shortcut to meetings by using the meeting ID. Use advanced meeting options, including encrypting meetings and cropping video.

Cisco Webex Meetings

Webex allows people to meet securely with integrated audio, video, and content sharing on any device. It provides online training, webinars, and remote support. Webex is available on any device—desktop, mobile, browser, and video system, and advertises a consistent user experience. A major draw to Webex is security strength. All plans include screen sharing, HD video, unlimited meetings, cloud recording and storage, and phone support during business hours. The free version has a limited number of participants. Plans provide more participants and technical support with higher pricing structures.

Pros: Integrates with many softwares and LMS systems, well suited for global organizations, easy to install and use.

Cons: High pricing structures and long turnarounds for technology support.

Accessibility: Keyboard accessibility, screen reader support, closed captioning and automated transcripts, interpreter integration, and custom layouts.

Tips and tricks: The capability for virtual backgrounds, adding polls to meetings, using meeting reports for relevant statistics, alternate hosts, and many other features are comparable with Zoom.

Crowdcast

Crowdcast is a multi-streaming platform for private use. It is interactive, supports webinars, and has the capabilities to reach any size audience and connect with your community.

Pros: Allows for different pricing levels depending on the event and has many interactive features, including polling, question and answers, and the ability to invite attendees on-screen.

Cons: A high learning curve and a complicated registration process.

Accessibility: Provides permissions for varying accessibility features.

From the field: "With Crowdcast you do not have the ability to be as interactive, but you can reach a larger audience due to the social networking aspect," said Janie Hermann, manager of adult programming at the Princeton Public Library in Princeton, New Jersey. "Crowdcast has a learning curve but is much less expensive than Zoom."

GoToMeeting

GoToMeeting enables face-to-face meetings and collaborations.

Pros: GoToMeeting boasts high-definition videoconferencing and speed with several popular features, including messaging and hand raising. Smart Meeting Transcription and Siri audio commands are helpful features. Switching from videoconferencing to chat along with call forwarding is user-friendly. Mobile features are constantly getting updated. Pricing plans offer various add-ons for additional features.

Cons: There are no free plan options, and there's limited storage availability in the cloud. Meetings with many attendees can have connection issues, and entering a meeting on a mobile device can prove difficult.

Accessibility: Features vary depending on the app. Keyboard shortcuts, high-contrast mode, and tab navigation are available.

Tips and tricks: Set up recurring meetings and make sure to do a precheck of audio and visual. Be sure to lock meetings to keep out unwanted guests.

Microsoft Teams

Designed for collaboration in the workplace, Microsoft Teams serves as a catch-all for workplace collaboration with strong videoconferencing tools. Teams helps organizations centralize products. All plans include a web version of Microsoft Office products, up to 300 users, and 24/7 support. Teams is available to businesses as part of Office 365 subscriptions and works easily with organizations that use the Microsoft Suite.

Pros: Integrates with Office applications including SharePoint and Word, and replaces Skype for Business. Integration is helpful for scheduling, specifically with Outlook calendars. Also, makes file sharing simple and convenient. Google Translate is available on messaging policies. There are organization-wide settings but also user-friendly guest access.

Cons: The combination of apps is confusing and takes a lot of memory and energy to run on computers (specifically Macs). Limited flexibility with cameras and microphones and few avenues for customization can prove difficult.

Accessibility: Live closed captioning, screen reader support, keyboard shortcuts, ability to reduce background noise, easily add an interpreter or coworker to a call, customizable reading and viewing features, Immersive Reader to break down text, text telephones, and dark, light, and high-contrast themes.

Tips and tricks: Search through past conversations for information, send and filter messages by using @mention, use "do not disturb functions" to limit alerts, and blur your background. *Note:* Skype for Business was discontinued in July 2021 with recommendation that users move to Microsoft Teams.

From the field: Heather Hedderman, a STEAM teacher-librarian at Wattsburg Area School District in Wattsburg, Pennsylvania, likes creating a variety of channels in one space for her third and fourth graders. She prefers Seesaw for grades K–2 because it is more visually appealing and easier to navigate.

TEXTBOX 6.1

Janie Hermann, manager of adult programming at the Princeton Public Library in Princeton, New Jersey, shares her perspectives on multiple videoconferencing platforms.

"We have experimented and used a variety of platforms over the last two years, but the three that we use most frequently are Zoom, Crowdcast, and Google Meet. Zoom and Google Meet are very similar, and once people realize this, they quickly become comfortable using either platform. We like the interactive aspects that can be achieved when using meeting mode with Zoom and Meet as well as the screen-sharing ability, the use of breakout rooms, and the option of having webinar mode when needed for a presentation or session."

Google Meet (through Google Hangouts)

The video communication that replaced Google Hangouts (along with Google Chat), Google Meet offers easy-to-join video calls with multiple users. Anyone with a Google account can create a video meeting, invite up to one hundred participants, and meet for up to one hour. Google Meet uses the same security protections as Google products and has live captions, screen-sharing capabilities, and can join from any device without necessary downloads.

Pros: Crisp audio and video, compatibility with most devices, and uses the cloud.

Cons: Limited customization on mobile, limited free features, limited recording abilities. *Accessibility:* Google Meet can integrate accessibility features from Meet (live captions), Chrome browser (screen readers), and Google meeting (room hardware).

Tips and tricks: Cast your meeting to another display, make use of all features, and change your video definition if there are connectivity issues. There's a Mute Tab extension, where you can open all breakout rooms in a browser, then unmute and mute them individually so you can listen and participate but don't have to hear all the noise at once.

From the field: "We like the interactive aspects that can be achieved when using meeting mode with Zoom and Meet as well as the screen-sharing ability, the use of breakout rooms, and the option of having webinar mode when needed for a presentation or session," Hermann said.

Zoom

Zoom is one of the most versatile videoconferencing applications, with video meetings, voice, webinars, and chat across all devices and spaces. Paid options offer more functionalities. Additional features include: Zoom Meetings & Chat, Zoom Phone, Zoom Video Webinars, Zoom Rooms & Conference Room Connector. Plans range from free to premium and licensed accounts, which have more features.

Pros: Accessibility to most people, user-friendly, high-quality audio and video.

Cons: Past security bugs deter users, limited features on the mobile app, and potential connectivity issues. For a more comprehensive look at Zoom, see chapter 7.

Additional videostreaming platforms include Amazon Chime (audio and videoconferencing), Zoho Meeting (video software that can pair well with other Zoho products), JoinMe (cloud-based conferencing with a free trial and monthly rates), ClickMeeting (specializes in large webinars), Facebook Messenger Rooms (video meeting technology), and StarLeaf (customizable videoconferencing that features business-wide connectivity).

As shown by Juana M. Flores, a senior librarian at the Kings Highway Branch of the Brooklyn Public Library, combining platforms can achieve a higher potential. "I have used Facebook, YouTube, and Zoom. There are many benefits for using all three. My ultimate favorite is using Facebook Live, especially with your phone. It is quick and easy to use via phone. The upside is once you're done, you can share with other groups with

---

TEXTBOX 6.2

A perspective on switching videoconferencing platforms from Melanie Taylor Coombs, adult services supervisor/librarian at McArthur Library in Biddeford, Maine.

"When the pandemic first prompted closure, we turned to the free platform Jitsi. It has been very successful for our virtual Knitting Program because it is very simple to use and requires no additional software. We use Zoom for professional meetings and larger programs. The Maine State Library organized free Zoom accounts for all public libraries. This platform has been preferable for programs that we record and post to YouTube and/or social media.

"Think about your users before you begin. When we migrated programming to Zoom, we first needed to teach novice patrons how to successfully use Zoom. That often required a phone call and step-by-step instructions. We developed several handouts that we would send out prior to one-on-one technology assistance. Then, we would often follow up. The pandemic forced many into using software they were not familiar with. We had to start where the patrons needed to start and be flexible in our approach."

the Internet. You also can use Facebook Live to attract more participants to your Zoom programs. The downside is you only have forty-eight hours to air it, and if you want to have higher viewership, you have to share with various Facebook groups."

Erin Weaver, the assistant director at the Bridgeville Public Library in Bridgeville, Pennsylvania, recommends using a variety of videostreaming platforms. "The library uses Zoom, Discord, Facebook Live, YouTube, Instagram, and Twitter," Weaver said. "Facebook Live is used for our virtual story times and allows us to present in real time, reaching families that may not yet be comfortable venturing out to in-person story time.

"I would recommend Zoom for online programming. It's versatile and you can use it for children-adult programs. We recently had a children's program that was originally scheduled for in-person but received no registrations. We moved it to Zoom and people signed up. Our children's librarian said that she could see some folks actually finishing dinner as the program began. I think that the convenience of this option works for a number of folks."

⑥ Other Digital Options and Video Editing

Separate from specific LMS and web-conferencing tools, there are other digital options for online instruction. Many of these options can help increase access for those who use less technology and can supplement and pair with the above technologies.

Videos can grab the attention of learners, be they promotional materials, wrap-ups, or in asynchronous learning. Prerecording, with an option for multiple takes, puts less pressure on staff for a perfect "first take." It also allows staff to record multiple programs per session, which can be helpful with limited access to equipment and space. Recording a program for future posting allows the provider to perfect their craft at their own pace and on their own schedule. On the other side, you need to evaluate how much time you want to spend re-filming and editing videos. Turnaround time is especially important to consider if multiple people take part in the production process. Large video files can take a long time to upload and send to others. You can share videos through web-based sharing options, flash drives and hard drives, or workplace cloud systems.

TEXTBOX 6.3 TIPS ON FILMING VIDEOS FOR EASIER EDITING

Nicole Lawton, a children's librarian at the Naperville Public Library in Naperville, Illinois, provides tips for filming a video for easier editing in the long run.

"If you are prerecording a program, do it in short segments and have a sign (I just wrote the name of the song, book, or action rhyme on scrap paper and held it up to the camera) so you know what segment it is for the editing process. Short segments help with video editing but also help if you make a mistake because you can just refilm it. If you are doing a programming series that is prerecorded, film a handful of short segments that can be mixed and matched so that you don't have to do twice the work. Let's face it, we are all exhausted and this way you can take the easy road."

Editing videos in advance can make the content more accessible for users by adding captions and clear transitions. Video editors add clips from around the world, screenshots from websites and book pages, and permissions for works used. Introduction and conclusion slides and graphics create consistent marketing. Some programs allow you to broadcast a pre-recorded video, "live."

Additional video-editing programs include Adobe Premiere, Animoto, DaVinci Resolve, and Moovly. Major deciding factors for video-editing software are computer capabilities and budget.

Facebook Live

Facebook Live uses a computer camera to livestream a video onto Facebook. The live-streaming feature pairs with Zoom or other video programs and can reach a larger audience. Facebook can send notifications to followers so they know to tune in at the right time.

Julia Frederick, an early literacy librarian at the Vernon Area Public Library in Lincolnshire, Illinois, broadcasts a weekly story time on Facebook Live. "I enjoy doing story time on Facebook Live because I know folks can then watch my story time at their leisure. I do still get engagement from patrons when they type their names or answer questions in the comment section, but I don't get to see their faces, which I don't like as much," Frederick said.

Facebook also automatically records live videos. This action potentially causes a copyright issue. Nicole Lawton, a children's librarian at the Naperville Public Library in Naperville, Illinois, posted short videos onto social media. They were three-to-five-minute snippets that showcased an un-copyrighted action rhyme, song, or flannel board activity. "It really boosted our social media numbers and engagement and was better utilized than our fifteen-to-twenty-minute story-time videos," Lawton said.

YouTube

YouTube provides a free livestream from webcams, mobiles, and encoders. The options for listed or unlisted content can keep information private and people can follow an organization's channel and look at past videos. Content can get lost in the massive stream of information. You can collect and upload videos and set up a channel and playlist to share and easily access your videos.

The YouTube platform is popular and well-known, with easy indexing. Cons include over-popularity, meaning videos can get lost easily, and advertising is a part of the free video benefits.

Frank Skornia, a digital librarian in Information & Adult Services at the Ferguson Library in Stamford, Connecticut, enjoyed focusing on YouTube over Zoom.

> During the period that the library was not offering in-person programming, I would offer a large portion of technology curriculum as livestreams on YouTube. I chose to use YouTube for a few different reasons. The first was access: It is easy to share the link to the streamed video, and anyone can access it in any browser without an account or installing an application. People are also familiar with YouTube's interface. The second reason is that I personally was familiar with how to set up livestreaming to a service like YouTube and knew that I could quickly adapt my teaching materials to be used in a livestream. Additionally, the library was putting effort into growing its online presence on YouTube, so

it fit well with the other projects being done by the library. Finally, by choosing a mostly unidirectional platform, I felt that I was able to avoid a lot of the problems that had been observed in the early days of the pandemic on platforms like Zoom, with folks unfamiliar with the technology and their devices or trolls disrupting meetings.

Niche Academy

Niche Academy works primarily for online training but also to share programming videos. The closed environment can keep access to certain people and reduce copyright concerns.

Lawton said, "I liked that Niche Academy was a private platform that our patrons could access so they could tune in to Storytime during a time that fit their schedule."

Other potential video programs for on-the-fly promotions and shorts include Vimeo and Metacafe. TikTok is a popular social media tool for short videos between five and sixty seconds long. iMovie comes for free on Mac, and Windows computers have varying video editors depending on your software version. Adobe Spark Video is free in the web browser once you create an account. It is a user-friendly video-training tool with the ability to search for copyright-free images and video. Biteable is a resource for on-the-spot videos. It can create fast and quick videos with limited special features. The free version includes watermarks.

Putting It Together

Many of the above-listed platforms are compatible with one another. There may be participants who are only comfortable using a specific platform and become intimidated by something new. Using multiple programs can help reach additional participants. It's also helpful to poll your participants for a specific program or meeting and see what works best for them. You might find that for a book club, one interface works a lot better than department meetings, a large program, or an intimate story time. It's important to evaluate the individual program and audience to see what platform will best suit your needs. Static media sites like Facebook groups, Slack, or Goodreads can provide central hubs for online instruction and conversation and promote and share video content.

Key Points

- There are a large number of web platforms to choose from when leading an environment. Evaluate your needs and those of your audience.
- Remember that it is okay to change platforms and to use more than one platform.
- Features are constantly changing, so make sure to consult the specific organization for the most up-to-date information.

Notes

1. "Behind the Blackboard!" accessed October 4, 2021, https://blackboard.secure.force.com/apex/publickbarticleview?id=kAA1O000000Kz2B&homepage=true.

2. Canvas Community, "What Are the Canvas Accessibility Standards?" Instructure Community, September 30, 2021, https://community.canvaslms.com/t5/Canvas-Basics-Guide/What-are-the-Canvas-accessibility-standards/ta-p/1564.

3. "Classroom | Google for Education," Google Classroom (Google), accessed November 3, 2021, https://edu.google.com/products/classroom/.

4. "Documentation," About Moodle—MoodleDocs, accessed October 3, 2021, https://docs.moodle.org/311/en/About_Moodle.

5. "The Most Comprehensive K-12 Teaching and Learning Suite," Schoology, accessed October 3, 2021, https://www.schoology.com/k-12.

Zoom

THIS CHAPTER FOCUSES SOLELY ON ZOOM because it is one of the most widely used interfaces for online instruction. At the onset of COVID-19, Zoom beat many of the technology giants with its ease of use, video quality, and connectivity.[1] Zoom has grown to enable the hybrid workforce through videoconferencing, chat, events, webinars, and beyond. I have done job interviews on Zoom, attended countless meetings, had family gift exchanges, attended a magic show, tutored children, toured my mom's closet, hosted a virtual field trip to China, and presented to five hundred librarians nationwide.

The platform makes things easy for users, and so many people have adopted it that there is a high familiarity level. People can access Zoom on a computer, tablet, or phone. No download is necessary for the most basic of usages.

Features vary between paid and free options and links can stay the same for multiple sessions. In this chapter, I highlight various Zoom plans, features, tips, and tricks. Universities, K–12 schools, and other large-scale organizations may have different restrictions and capabilities with their Zoom accounts.

Zoom achieved worldwide popularity because of its ease of use at the onset of the COVID-19 pandemic. Despite early security issues, the platform rallied and continues to offer up-to-date features for users.[2]

Presenters and participants can control many options to make the instructing and learning environment more comfortable. Helpful features for presentations include screen sharing, breakout rooms, polls, subtitles, group chats, interactive boards, waiting rooms, and appearance touch-up. The ability for interaction and customizability is part of what makes Zoom so popular.

"I love being able to interact with the children and grown-ups that attend story time," said Julia Frederick, early literacy librarian at the Vernon Area Public Library in Lincolnshire, Illinois. "I can see everyone's faces (if they choose) and we are able to communicate via shaker eggs, color sticks, fingers (with counting, giving each other high fives through the camera, etc.). Zoom is my favorite way to do story time."

Zoom is constantly changing and offering additional updates to make it more user-friendly. Check with the client for what features exist at your time of presentation. On a desktop you can check for updates by clicking on your profile photo. On a mobile, Zoom will display a notification whenever a new update is available. There are three types of updates: web-only for new fixes, mandatory updates where you cannot continue with Zoom until it is updated, and optional updates that require clicking on the update to begin. It's important to check for updates before a presentation, to prevent potential delays.

The Basics

Create a meeting: A title, date and time, and duration is mandatory to create a new meeting in Zoom. Optional fields include a description, frequency for recurring meetings, registration, meeting passwords, and alternative hosts. The optional fields help make information clearer for participants, manage security, and provide a backup plan if one host is unavailable. A scheduled meeting generates a unique meeting ID, which expires after thirty days without use.

Joining a meeting: Instructors need to open Zoom and click "Launch a meeting" through the meeting tab. Attendees can click the direct link to the meeting or enter the meeting ID after tapping "Join a meeting" on the Zoom homepage. Desktop computers have the most available features, though mobile devices and tablets work too.

Meeting settings: When you create a meeting, you have several choices. For security and safety, I recommend adding a meeting password, leaving the video off at logon for the host and participants, and allowing telephone and computer audio. Under advanced options you can choose to mute participants on entry and record the meeting in the cloud. Advanced options are also where you can designate an alternate host.

Record a meeting: The "Record a meeting" option is available in the bottom right corner of the screen. Press this button to start the recording. Only the host can record a meeting. To automatically record all meetings, you can select Meeting Settings from your main account, click "Recording," and choose an option called "Automatic Recording." This option is helpful because a common mistake is to forget to press the record button. Attendees receive a message that Zoom is recording the meeting, and phone attendees will receive an audio notification, which helps alleviate any security concerns.

Recording a meeting is beneficial for people who cannot attend, if someone wants to watch themselves presenting, and for accessibility so people can view something on their own time and stop and start the recording at their own pace.

Chat: Zoom's chat feature is an easy way for participants to interact without disrupting the session. However, some may find it distracting or that attendees misuse it. The

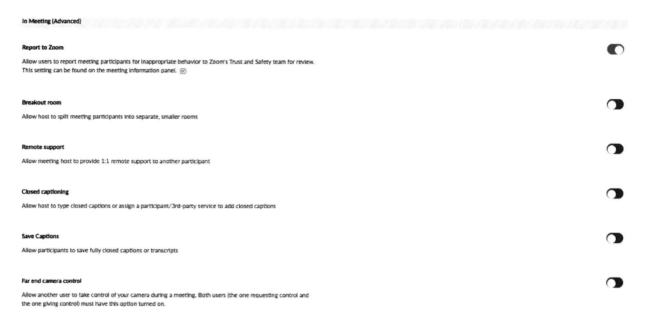

In Meeting (Advanced)

Report to Zoom

Allow users to report meeting participants for inappropriate behavior to Zoom's Trust and Safety team for review. This setting can be found on the meeting information panel. ✓

Breakout room

Allow host to split meeting participants into separate, smaller rooms

Remote support

Allow meeting host to provide 1:1 remote support to another participant

Closed captioning

Allow host to type closed captions or assign a participant/3rd-party service to add closed captions

Save Captions

Allow participants to save fully closed captions or transcripts

Far end camera control

Allow another user to take control of your camera during a meeting. Both users (the one requesting control and the one giving control) must have this option turned on.

Figure 7.1. Advanced Zoom meeting settings. *Zoom*

host has the ability to turn off the chat feature by selecting the additional drop-down in the lower left of the chat box. Options are that participants can chat with:

- No one
- Hosts and co-hosts
- Everyone (in public forum)
- Everyone and anyone directly (private messaging)

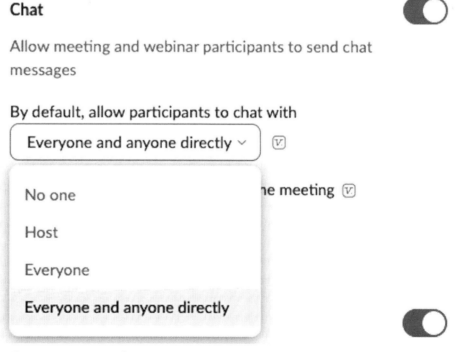

Figure 7.2. Zoom chat options. *Zoom*

Private chats are helpful for troubleshooting and off-topic information, but it is important to note that private chats are visible for all to see in the chat transcript.

Hosts and co-hosts: The host can start and stop the Zoom class, assign screen-sharing privileges, stop videos, and remove students. Additional privileges include enabling security measures, viewing meeting participants, sharing screens, setting up a live transcript, choosing reaction options, setting up polls and breakout rooms, and ending the meeting. The host can also assign a co-host once the session has begun, or designate an alternate host before the session.

Co-hosts can help manage participants and recording but cannot start meetings, livestreams, breakout rooms, polls, closed captioning, or waiting rooms. They can move participants from the waiting room. See table 7.1 for a chart breaking down privileges of hosts, co-hosts, and participants.

Table 7.1   General Zoom Permissions

ACTION	HOST	CO-HOST	PARTICIPANT
Answer Poll			X
Ask Poll	X	X	
Chat	X	X	X
Designate Co-Host	X		
End Meeting	X		
File Sharing	X	X	X
Lock Meeting	X	X	
Lock Screen Sharing	X	X	
Modify Meeting Settings	X	X	
Mute/Unmute All	X	X	
Raise Hand			X
Remove Attendee	X	X	
Share Video	X	X	
Stop Video	X	X	

Hosts and co-hosts have a great deal of authority, which is helpful in monitoring situations. "I feel like I have a decent amount of control over how we engage with our participants, making it as smooth an experience as possible," Julie Zimmerman, children's librarian at the Brooklyn Public Library in Brooklyn, New York, said.

Mute, mute, mute: If a person is not speaking, their mute button should be on, even if they are a co-presenter. Muting helps prevent unwanted feedback and background noise and makes it easier for everyone to hear. Muting everyone when they enter a meeting and asking them to unmute is a way to avoid unwanted secondary noise.

The mute and "Unmute all" options are helpful for quick changes, along with keyboard shortcuts for rapid muting and unmuting. In Windows use *Alt* + *A*, and for Mac

Shift + Command + A. You can press and hold the space key to temporarily unmute yourself.

Participants can unmute themselves at any time. While hosts and co-hosts can lock screen sharing, they cannot lock audio sharing.

Lisa Mulvenna, head of children's and teen services at the Clinton-Macomb Public Library in Clinton Township, Michigan, enjoys the ability to interact with patrons on Zoom. "My favorite part is when the kids share their cameras and we can interact," Mulvenna said. "I also love that we are able to reach new participants in different ways, from whole school classes to bedtime stories in pajamas."

Personal meeting ID: All Zoom users receive a unique personal meeting ID that leads them to a private room. This ID is helpful for short meetings or practice sessions. However, if you constantly use the same ID, security may become compromised. The personal meeting ID will expire after 365 days without use.

Display settings: Possible display settings vary depending on what the presenter is doing. If no one is screen-sharing, the options are "Gallery view," which shows all users' profile images, or "Speaker view," which shows the image of the person currently speaking. You can also pin someone's image to the center of the view by right-clicking the blue button in the top right corner of their image and selecting "Pin."

During a story time, I like to pin the presenters' image so that the viewers can see the book and the speaker. If I am the host of a program, I prefer "Gallery view" so that I can see all the participants. "Speaker view" is helpful in meetings when you want to see who is speaking.

When a user is screen-sharing, the display options change. The first option is "Standard view," with shared content in the center of the screen and participants' images above. The second option is "Side-by-side gallery," where participants' images are on the right side of the content, and the third option is "Side-by-side speaker," which is similar to gallery but with only the speaker's image. The final option is "Swap video and share screen," where the image of the person is in the center and the content is where the images usually are.

The person sharing their screen will lose participants' images and chat unless they have multiple monitors or devices. To make them visible, select "More" at the end of the toolbar, "Chat" for the chat box, and "Show video panel" for the participants' images. If no cameras are on, the video panel option is not available. When presenting, I like to log on to Zoom on a second device so that I can see images and chat easier.

Ending a session: On the right side of your individual Zoom box is a button that says "End meeting," then "End meeting for all." You can select someone else to be the host

TEXTBOX 7.1

Lisa Jones, youth services librarian at the West Osceola Library in Celebration, Florida, offers tips for a smooth-running Zoom session.

"Be sure to speak slowly. On Zoom, set up a waiting room and make sure that you mute everyone as they enter. Remind them to change their name as they may have signed on with someone else's account (especially if they are younger). Also, if multiple people are talking at one time, Zoom cuts out and you don't really hear any of them!"

and leave the meeting, or simply leave the meeting and Zoom selects a random person to be host. The recording stops when specifically selected, when the host selects "End meeting for all," or when everyone has exited the meeting.

Zoom Plans

Below is a general overview of the many different Zoom plan options. Please consult Zoom for the most recent features and pricing models. It is ideal to use an organization's Zoom account for instruction and an individual account only for personal use.

Basic: Host an unlimited number of meetings with up to one hundred participants for a maximum of forty minutes each. Chat with groups, send files, make breakout rooms, share single or multiple screens, and/or call into a meeting via Zoom.

Pro: All the basic features are available with meetings of up to thirty hours, ability to delegate meetings (another Pro user can set up meetings), storage for up to 1 GB of files, user management, and social media streaming.

Enterprise: All basic features with the additional hosting capabilities of up to five hundred participants with unlimited cloud storage.

Business: Host up to three hundred people, with single sign-on, transcripts of recordings, managed domains, and company branding. More than that, Zoom United Business includes a calling plan.

If there is at least one licensed user, all of the above plans have optional add-on features including audio conferencing, large meeting sizes, cloud storage, and additional support.

Other available options that are not typically used in libraries include Zoom phone with unlimited calling. Organizations can contact Zoom for specialized plans and offers to meet individual needs, including Zoom for Education.

Zoom Events and Webinar (previously Zoom Webinar) is often used in libraries, especially when trying to reach a large number of people with limited participation. The ordinary Zoom features exist with interactive video panelists and screen sharing, question and answers, practice sessions, post-event surveys, and recordings and transcripts. The number of attendees can range from five hundred to ten thousand and above. Webinars include unlimited sessions of up to thirty hours each, exportable attendee lists, marketing integration, paid registration, livestreaming, and engagement reports. Zoom Events expands on Webinars by enabling multi-session options, event hubs, networking, and event reporting. This feature is ideal for conferences and large-scale events.

Zoom Rooms consist of individual meeting rooms. This feature is more commonly used for businesses than teaching but could be helpful for large library institutions. *Zoom United* is a plan that adds phone options.

Key Features

Registration: Though not mandatory through Zoom, your organization may make a different decision. Registrations can make it simple to take attendance and send reminders and updates. Select "Registration" on the main meeting page.

Waiting room: A waiting room on Zoom is very similar to one in a doctor's office. It gives the instructor control of when the participants come in and can allow an instructor time to prepare the session. You can enable a waiting room through *advanced meeting options* in the web browser. From there, you can choose which participants automatically enter the waiting room and which do not.

Participant screen sharing: Participants can share their screens if given permissions from a host using the green "Share" button at the bottom of the Zoom window. One can share an entire computer screen, Zoom's whiteboard app, an iPhone or iPad connected to the same wireless network, or specific windows and programs open on the computer.

Advanced options include selecting a portion of the screen to share, sharing only sound, and sharing content from a second camera on your computer, for example, another webcam. To change your share, press the green "New Share" button, and to complete screen sharing, click the red "Stop Share" button. Phones, depending on the model, have limited capabilities to share audio and annotate. Make sure to be careful to mute unnecessary sounds and notifications when screen sharing.

"I prefer to use Zoom," Chelsea Corso, a children's librarian at the Barrett Paradise Friendly Library in Cresco, Pennsylvania, said. "I like that I can see the children and that they can see each other. I also prefer to screen-share e-books for virtual story times, and Zoom is a great way to do that."

Breakout rooms: You can create breakout rooms for intimate discussions and group work. You can create up to fifty breakout rooms with two hundred participants or less; however, you can only create as many rooms as the number of participants currently in the main Zoom room. The recording does not cover the breakout rooms. The host needs to manually move participants who join via their browser or phone into a breakout room.

Enable rooms in the advanced meeting sessions on the web browser before a session. Creation of breakout rooms happens after a session begins. Select breakout rooms, the number of rooms, and whether to manually or automatically split participants into rooms or allow participants to enter breakout rooms on their own. Another option is to pre-assign breakout rooms through the *Breakout Room Assignment* function. This function only works if participants log in with the same email address as registered with.

When you create the breakout rooms, you have the option to rename them and can click the gear icon for additional options, which include setting a time limit and countdown timer for the breakout rooms. If you choose to have breakout rooms close automatically, a timer displays on everyone's screen.

It is possible, but difficult, to pre-assign breakout rooms because participants need a Zoom account and to use that Zoom account. You can "allow participants to return to the main room" at any time. Users can select "Ask for help" and "Invite host" to the breakout room. Remember not to select "Leave the meeting" but to select "Leave the breakout room."

When in breakout rooms, the host can broadcast a message to all breakout rooms by selecting the option, or typing a message and then clicking "Broadcast." A host can jump between breakout rooms, and participants can ask for help from a breakout room.

The whiteboard is a feature often used in breakout rooms to collect participants' ideas in one place and then share with the larger group. The host needs to enable screen sharing for participants, so one participant can share a screen and select the whiteboard. All users should be able to automatically draw on the whiteboard, but an override is *More >Enable/ Disable Annotations for Others* in the toolbar at the bottom of your screen. Participants can annotate the whiteboard by selecting *View options > Annotate*.

To share the whiteboard with the main group, one person must press the "Save" button in the whiteboard toolbar and choose to save it as a PDF or PNG. After clicking "Save" a pop-up called *Show in folder* appears, and you can confirm where the image saved on your computer. If you're trying to locate the image, it is most likely in a folder named Zoom that the client automatically created. Once you open the whiteboard image on your screen, you can return to the main room and share your screen with the whiteboard image.

Polls: Hosts need to enable polls through a web browser before a session. From there, create polls before a session through upcoming meetings in the web browser or during a session in the Zoom window. The maximum number of polls for a meeting is twenty-five, and polls must have a question and at least two answers. You can select if a poll is anonymous or not.

I like to create polls in advance of a meeting and then add more if needed during or at the beginning of a session. During virtual field trips, I let attendees vote on our location to attend and in book clubs, users vote for what title to read next. Polls are a useful way to gauge prior knowledge and to find out how many people are attending a program.

During a class, select "Polls," then the poll you want, and launch polling. Participants receive prompts to complete questions, and the host sees the results in real time. The host can *end polling* and choose to *share the results*. Once finished, remember to *stop sharing* to take the poll off the screen or hide results.

Relaunching a poll deletes past results. To edit polls, the host clicks to create a new poll, and clicks on the poll to edit. The host can download poll results through the web browser on Pro accounts on the Usage Reports page.

"I like Zoom a lot because of the ability to conduct quick polls, its chat function, and the breakout rooms," Stephanie Dietrich, learning commons director at District 203 in Naperville, Illinois, said.

Extra Features

Phoning in: Some attendees may need to call into a meeting. Use the "Phone Call" tab on the top menu. The participant dials the numbers shown and enters the Meeting and Participant ID. If a participant does not know their ID, they can enter the pound sign.

Auto-saved chats: In basic meeting settings, you can choose to have all chats auto-saved to your automatically curated Zoom folder. I find that a lot of participants want to go back to the chat, especially from webinars and trainings, and look at all the ideas shared. It can be difficult to keep up with the chat, audio, and video during a live presentation.

Join from browser: In advanced meeting settings, you can select that participants automatically receive an option to join the Zoom meeting from their web browser. Participants may prefer this choice if they want to project the Zoom screen onto another monitor.

Live transcription: Zoom worked to have live transcription available to all users by 2021 but allowed people to request it before then. There is a *live transcript* option either automatically in your controls or after pressing the More button. You then should click it and enable auto-transcription. Zoom will auto-transcribe the audio. If you wish to hide the subtitles for yourself, you can click the ^ next to the *live transcript* button. You won't see the subtitles, but participants can. Transcription provides accessibility options for those hard of hearing, English as a Second Language Learners, and struggling or beginning readers.

"The features I use most often in Zoom are captioning. Though their captions are not always great, they are better than most," Carrie Banks, supervising librarian for Inclusive Services at the Brooklyn Public Library, said. "Live closed captioners I work with tell me that the interface is decent. The same is true for world language interpretation. The ability to easily pin an ASL interpreter is important."

Hand raising: Attendees can physically raise their hands, which involves viewing it through the monitor; can ask questions in the chat; or can use the "Raise Hand" function from the *Participants* icon at the bottom of their Zoom box. The participants' list goes down in the order they raised their hands, so you can call on specific students.

Nonverbal feedback: Reactions such as a raised hand or an emoji symbol allow participants to express feedback nonverbally. The three dots in the upper right corner allow you to select additional emojis to use as reactions. The emojis appear in the top left corner of users' images. The host can click "Participants," to see the counts of people using different reactions.

File sharing: To share a file in Zoom during a session, click on the chat, then the drop-down. Select "File," then choose a specific file to send to all or one participants. The participants will see the notification and can download the file.

Recording video: If you don't have a video-recording program on your computer you're comfortable with, you can use Zoom as a recording studio. Steps to record in Zoom are to start a new meeting and share your screen if you want the image to be more than your face. Then click the red record button and what location to save the recording in. Please note that there is a processing period after recording and after editing that can last for several hours. Plan accordingly.

After recording and exporting, find the video on your computer. Locations may vary but it is in a Zoom-created folder. Figure 7.3 shows how to determine where the video files save. From there, you can proceed with your video as desired.

Recordings: If you automatically record your sessions, you can access Zoom recordings by logging in to your Zoom account and viewing cloud recordings. If you record a meeting onto your computer, you can find the file through the Zoom folder on your device.

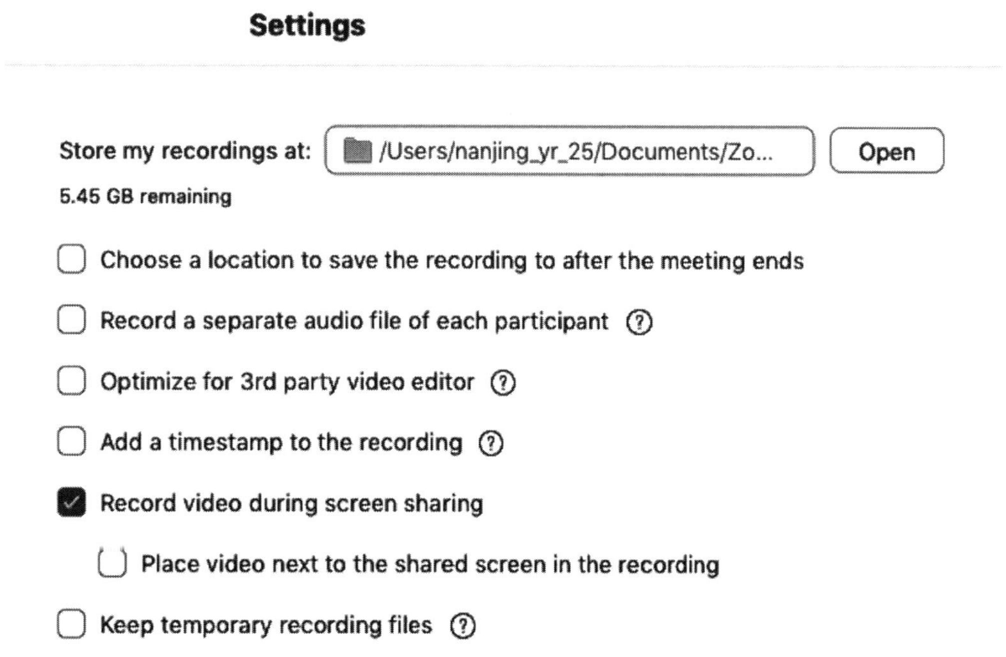

Settings

Store my recordings at: [📁 /Users/nanjing_yr_25/Documents/Zo...] [Open]

5.45 GB remaining

☐ Choose a location to save the recording to after the meeting ends

☐ Record a separate audio file of each participant ⑦

☐ Optimize for 3rd party video editor ⑦

☐ Add a timestamp to the recording ⑦

☑ Record video during screen sharing

    ☐ Place video next to the shared screen in the recording

☐ Keep temporary recording files ⑦

Figure 7.3. Zoom video-saving options. *Zoom*

Annotation: If given privileges, participants can mark up a presentation and annotate slides and visuals on the screen. I prefer to only use this feature in breakout rooms because, especially with younger crowds, I find they end up doodling on the screen.

Virtual backgrounds: To set up a virtual background, click the ^ next to the video icon in the Zoom toolbar and choose "Virtual Background." This option allows you to display an image as your background and is helpful for consistency or privacy but also may provide distractions to participants. If you don't remove your virtual background before ending a meeting, it will remain as a default for the next meeting. To remove it, return to choose "Virtual Background," and select "None."

Other: Helpful features available under "Other" in settings include *blur snapshot on IOS app switcher*, which can blur your screen content when screen sharing. *Schedule privilege* gives others the ability to schedule meetings with your account.

Ⓢ Additional Features

Beyond the basics, there are many additional features available on Zoom. You can locate many through settings on the Zoom client, and enable more through a web browser. Special features add security, interactivity, and advanced options. Take time to experiment with the special features and see what would work best with your needs. The personal meeting room is helpful for experimentation. Some libraries hold Zoom office hours where users can practice with Zoom.

Ⓢ Tips and Tricks

Practice makes perfect: Even if you have used Zoom a million times before, it never hurts to test all features in advance. Here's a sample checklist of a practice session in Zoom.

1. Test all audio and video devices. Mute and unmute yourself and turn your video off and on.
2. Open your participants list and click through the options, including *mute* and *unmute all.*
3. Practice sharing your screen, sharing a file, and posting a reaction. Try sharing your desktop, a specific screen, a document, and the whiteboard. Use *share* and *stop share* to practice transitions.
4. Create a sample poll question.
5. Investigate different views including *gallery*, *side-by-side*, and *presenter* to see what format works best. Also, practice pinning and unpinning a specific speaker.
6. If other people are with you, practice creating and sending them to breakout rooms.

Nothing's working: Common issues in Zoom can include video or audio not working properly. Enable your audio and camera through Settings in Zoom, and if using a web browser, enable the camera and audio settings through the web browser's preferences.

Alternative hosts: Designate an alternative host when creating a meeting. The alternate host needs a license on the same account. This person can start a session if the host is unavailable.

Clear all feedback: Wipes out all nonverbal reactions when you need a clean slate.

Quick troubleshooting ideas: Technology issues are going to happen in Zoom and some quick troubleshooting ideas are to turn Airplane mode off and on, and restart the Internet browser, Zoom, and your device.

Struggling to find a meeting ID: Many organizations reuse meeting IDs for multiple sessions. If you are unable to find the information for a meeting ID, you can go to your Zoom account and *join meeting* and see your past ten meeting room IDs.

Keyboard shortcuts: The Zoom website lists an extensive number of keyboard shortcuts (https://support.zoom.us/hc/en-us/articles/205683899-hot-keys-and-keyboard-for-zoom).

You can view and edit keyboard shortcuts in accessibility settings. Some of the most commonly used shortcuts are:

For Mac devices:

- Command (⌘) + W: Close the current window.
- Command (⌘) + L: Switch to portrait or landscape view, depending on the current view.
- Ctrl + T: Switch from one tab to the next.

And for Windows devices:

- F6: Navigate between Zoom popup windows.
- Ctrl + Alt + Shift: Move focus to Zoom's meeting controls.

Zoom status: An easy way to tell if the problem is your technology or Zoom is checking the Zoom status web page: https://status.zoom.us.

Saving chats: Oftentimes, instructors cannot address all questions in the chat during the allotted time, or people would like to reference the chat. The More button has an option to save the chat as a text file.

Minimizing Zoom: If you are in full-screen mode, you cannot minimize Zoom. Press *ESC* on your keyboard to exit full-screen mode. You can click into another program to completely minimize Zoom but still hear the audio. To return to the main Zoom room, click the Zoom icon on your toolbar. The other option is to click the Minimize button in the top right corner of your screen to create a miniature version of Zoom and still see the video. Click the green button in the bottom right corner to return to the main screen.

Discipline: If you're having an issue with someone, options can include moving them to a breakout room for a private conversation, muting them, or turning off their video. The presenter also has the ability to remove someone from the room.

Time zone: If your meeting times do not seem correct, there may be a time zone issue. Log in to Zoom and from your profile, select "Edit," and make sure to select the correct time zone.

Unauthorized user: If you try to log in to a Zoom meeting and receive an "unauthorized user" error message, it is likely that it is a secure Zoom organization and you need to log on using SSO information.

I have found myself unable to enter classrooms because I did not have an organizational Zoom account. The teachers had to work with technical support in advance to make sure access was available.

Dual monitors: From settings in the top left corner, you can choose General and "Use dual monitors." This setting allows you to share your screen on one monitor and view participants and chat on the other.

Invitations: You can invite participants to a meeting by sharing the meeting room code and Zoom link, copying the meeting information from Zoom, or clicking the shield in the right-hand corner of your screen during an active meeting and copying and sharing the Zoom link.

"I like the amount of control I have and the ease of sending out invites on my end and the ease of accepting on parents' end," Caitlin Snyder, branch team lead at the Cincinnati and Hamilton County Public Library in Cincinnati, Ohio, said. "I also love having the ability to mute my audience. Screen sharing is also paramount for my non–story time crowds (library instruction for middle and high school students)."

Zoom integrated apps: The Zoom App Marketplace introduces products to integrate into Zoom and launch tools from within the client. Categories include analytics, archiving, CRM, Carrier, Collaboration, Customer Service, Education, Event Management, Finance, Games, Healthcare, Learning and Development, Lifestyle, Marketing, Monitoring, PeopleOps, Productivity, Recording, Sales, Scheduling, Security and Compliance, Telehealth, and Transcriptions. Applications are exclusive to Zoom like Jenkins, Timer, and Virtual Backgrounds or integrated from already popular apps like Kahoot, Heads Up, and Mentimeter.

Security

Particularly in the beginning days of the government shutdown, Zoom security options were lax, leading to something known as Zoom bombing, where trespassers take over meetings with pornographic content, offensive images, and hate speech. Other Zoom security concerns included phishing scams to steal someone's Zoom account, and false end-to-end encryption claims. These incidents soured the Zoom experience for many, however, the company worked to put proper security measures in place to prevent ongoing incidents. Many of the additional features help presenters have more control over their meetings.

The "waiting room" function requires participants to enter a separate room before the session starts. This function provides staff an opportunity to check names against attendance lists and message or block unwanted participants. In the security options, the host can lock the meeting, disable the chat function, determine whether users can unmute themselves, and remove or report participants. Password protection is another way to make sure accounts are extra secure.

Additional available features include *Suspend participant activities*, which pauses the meeting, kicks out disruptive participants, and then resumes the meeting; and *Report by participants*, which allows meeting participants to report disruptive participants.

Requiring attendees to turn their camera on or put in their last name may help with security but also can invade privacy. Some instructors ask attendees to quickly turn their cameras off and on, or to enter their first name and last initial. There is also an option to stop members from saving chat if you do not want a meeting or chat recorded.

Your organization may have security features that are either automatically enabled or required. Some schools have functions where only people with a school account can access Zoom. These functions can prove problematic when attempting to let in guest speakers.

Emily Hampston, adult services coordinator at the Palos Park Public Library in Palos Park, Illinois, shares some tips and tricks for security while using Zoom.

"Zoom allows for privacy and a secure connection. Screen sharing is very useful and you can mute participants. Make sure you explain your policy on muting and cameras on/off at the beginning. For registration, collect information in the format of a standard program instead of just giving out the Zoom link. This can prevent Zoom bombers. Create a video and written tutorial explaining how to open a Zoom program and promote these resources (especially to older patrons). You can 'pin' the screen that you want to be the largest. This is useful for watching presenters."

The *Lock meeting* option prevents new participants from joining the meeting, even if they know the information.

Accessibility

"Up to 25 percent of your audience has a disability, and you want to make sure they are able to access and understand the information you are providing," Banks said. "I use Zoom because people are familiar with it, and its options are better than most."

Zoom provides many customized accessibility options.[3] Zoom's accessibility features include:

- Live transcription, manual captions, and third-party captioning options.
- Multi-spotlight, multi-pinning, and Rearrange Gallery view.
- Font-size customization, keyboard shortcuts, and screen reader support.
- Voicemail transcription and text formatting.
- Dark mode and focus mode.

Find detailed accessibility information in chapter 10.

Downsides of Zoom

Aside from Zoom bombing and security, one of the biggest pitfalls of Zoom is often the view when in presenter mode. It can be difficult to see attendees while sharing a screen or in presenter mode. There is an option to split the screen so attendees are seeing your shared screen, and you see them. Search for *Side by Side Mode for Screen Sharing* in Zoom's help center. Additional workarounds include using a multiple screen setup or logging on to Zoom from two separate devices.

Other downsides include:

- The subscriptions and add-ons on Zoom are cumbersome and too much for organizations with small budgets or personal users.

- The inability to delete inappropriate chat comments on the fly. (You can edit the chat transcription after a session.)
- For full functionality, users need to download the Zoom app.
- The cloud video sizes are inconsistent and can take up a lot of spaces.

Any videoconferencing platform has its drawbacks, and it is important to evaluate the pros and cons to decide what is best for your organization.

Frequently Asked Questions

Do my attendees need a paid Zoom account?
As long as the person hosting a meeting is from a paid Zoom account, participants can access the paid features.

Do I use the same Zoom account for everything?
Organizations may have specific logins for professional accounts, and schools oftentimes have special Zoom accounts for their organizations. Consult the documents for the organization you are working with. These would have a special login page or access through the Zoom SSO login page.

Can I use Zoom through a web browser?
Yes, Zoom works through a web browser with limited capabilities. Screen sharing may lag, you can only see one video stream at a time, and attendees cannot participate in polls or join a breakout room.

Am I able to host multiple meetings at once?
Hosts are able to schedule and attend two meetings at once. Enable this setting through the Zoom web browser in settings, then "Join different meetings simultaneously on desktop."

Key Points

- Familiarize yourself with the features and options of various Zoom plans.
- Make sure to practice any features you want to use in Zoom before a presentation.
- One of the benefits of Zoom is the user simplicity and capacity for interaction.
- Make sure your Zoom sessions are secure to prevent any unwanted guests.

Notes

1. Shannon Bond, "A Pandemic Winner: How Zoom Beat Tech Giants to Dominate Video Chat," NPR (NPR, March 19, 2021), www.npr.org/2021/03/19/978393310/a-pandemic-winner-how-zoom-beat-tech-giants-to-dominate-video-chat.
2. Lily Howell, "One Year on, Is Zoom Safe to Use?" Growth Through Technology, March 19, 2021, www.netitude.co.uk/blog/one-year-on-is-zoom-safe-to-use.
3. "Accessibility," Zoom, October 27, 2021, https://explore.zoom.us/en/accessibility/.

Evaluating and Recommending Resources

I INTRODUCED MANY RESOURCES DURING THE FIRST seven chapters of this book. For every type of online work and presentation, there is a tool or add-on that can go with it. Some of these add-ons are amazing and can bring your presentation to the next level, while others might overload your presentation. It is easy to get very excited about a new resource and want to show it to everybody, or to be overwhelmed about the scope of resources and never use anything new. Try to take a systematic approach. Start with your needs and see what applications may help you. Don't hesitate to play around with new resources if you have the time and energy. I like to test them out with my family and friends before using them on a professional level. Integrating apps into a livestream program is difficult, but more and more applications are partnering with certain livestreams.

Evaluating Resources

The vast number of supplemental resources is extremely overwhelming. I will break down some of the best resources and you can see what can serve your needs. Resources are constantly changing and getting updated. Compatibilities and availability may have changed since the publication of this book, so make sure to check with the direct source for up-to-date information.

Also, remember not to bog down your presentation with additional elements. Before deciding to use something, test it out, ask yourself what the purpose is, and see if the resource improves your presentation. Think about the education problem that the tool addresses and solves. Your chosen resources depend on your organization's capacity, goals, and community.

When choosing and evaluating resources, I find the "Read, Reflect, Display, and Do (R2D2)" model, introduced by Curtis Bonk and Ke Zhang, helpful.[1] You can think about what resource you want to use and which category or categories it falls into. This thinking ensures you have a well-rounded approach. The method you use makes a difference in how you present content, promote active learning, keep learning social, and help students engage. It's also important to be flexible and remember that what engages one learner may not engage another.

You should also think about your community, if your resources are in line with their interests and needs, how they adapt to various devices, what software is necessary to use the resources, and how the resources can work for different age groups and users at your organization.

Recommended Resources

I will break down resources into different categories with two or three recommended resources and quick explanations so you can determine what to try with your users. Many tools (especially the highest-quality ones) are versatile and can fit into several categories. For a fully comprehensive view, please visit the individual tool's provider. This guide provides a snapshot of options and possibilities. I begin with the basic definition of popular resources and expand from there.

Take a look, see what you might like, and practice with it to see if it fits your needs. If it doesn't, continue exploring in the category to find the right fit. I like searching for the broad category and typing a resource, followed by substitutes or alternatives, into a search engine.

Accessibility Resources/Extensions

Accessible means easily used or accessed by people with disabilities. Accessibility is ensuring websites, resources, and files are available to and usable by as many people as possible See chapter 10 for detailed explanations of accessibility and additional resources. There are many resources available that can help users of all abilities read and access technology.

WebAnywhere is a free web-based screen reader for all operating systems and web browsers. *Read&Write* is a text-to-speech program that provides visual and auditory text feedback. *Rev* provides automatic live captions for livestreaming platforms.

Asynchronous Communication

In asynchronous communication, people exchange information independent of time. Examples include emails, online forums, and collaborative documents. *Slack* is a messaging app with team dashboards and multiple channels for communication. Plans begin at free and also offer paid versions with more options. *Marco Polo* is a video-messaging app that's sometimes called a video walkie-talkie. *Google Docs*, part of the Google Suite, is an online word processor where you can create and format documents with others. The ability to see past versions and changes is quite helpful. *Discord* is a free voice, video, and chat app for ages thirteen and up that small networks use, commonly for gaming.

"We created a teen-gaming Discord that connects our teens to those across the county," Erin Weaver, assistant director at the Bridgeville Public Library in Bridgeville, Pennsylvania, said. "They've loved meeting new teens and making friends. Our teen librarian (Youth Services Specialist) collaborated with librarians from multiple libraries to create a county-wide Discord server for teens. Its primary function is to connect teens that enjoy gaming, but they experimented with offering homework help on it as well."

Other helpful applications for asynchronous communication include Google Forms, Seesaw, Flipgrid, and Padlet.

Avatars

An avatar is an icon or figure that represents a unique person either as a lifelike representation or a cartoon character. They can personify people without using personal images, which helps people have a sense of security. Make sure to check restrictions for the specific avatar program. *Cartoonify* is a free avatar generator where you can create an avatar with specific features, save it, and use it on social media. *Bitmoji* is a popular web and phone app and integrates with many popular applications. It enhances a character with many poses and outfits. The avatar creator is very versatile, and one can create Bitmoji classrooms to showcase digital resources. *Boo* allows users to create a full-body 3D avatar with various skin tones, clothes, and beyond.

Blogs

Blogs are a regularly updated website or web page, typically run by an individual or small group and read by many people, written in a conversational style. Posts are displayed in chronological order. In 2004, *blog* was one of Merriam-Webster's words of the year. Blogs function for user reflections, updates, and sharing information.

There are countless platforms for blogs and one should do individual research on what works best for their specific needs. Most blogging sites are free, but you need to pay for an individual domain name. *WordPress* is an open-source blogging platform, which provides free themes, images, and plug-ins, that are search engine friendly. *Wix* is a website platform that allows you to add a blog to the web page, and *Blogger* is Google's free blogging service that has few tools but is reliable and secure. Other blogging platforms include *Tumblr*, *Medium*, *Squarespace*, and *Weebly*.

Critical Thinking

Commonly used for education, many apps can use critical thinking in unique ways through the digital format. *Rationale* is an app that creates online argument maps *Google Fusion Tables* enters a new level of filtering and summarizing spreadsheets.

Calendar and Scheduling

Shared applications for calendars and scheduling can help people find an ideal meeting time that fits a large group. *SignUpGenius* allows you to create a schedule with open time slots and auto-reminders. *Calendly* has meeting sign-up with automatic integration to online calendars and videoconferencing platforms like Zoom, and *Doodle* is an online calendar tool for scheduling meetings.

Chrome Extensions (also featured in Chapter 6: Choosing a Platform)

Google Chrome extensions are additional programs installed into Chrome to modify the functionality by adding new features or modifying the behavior of the web browser. Many extensions can be beneficial, but some may be malicious and bring spam into your computer. Make sure to evaluate any extension before downloading. Many helpful tools are available to integrate as a Chrome Extension including but not limited to *Screencastify*, *Tab Scissors*, *Tab Glue*, *Web Paint*, *Share to Classroom*, *Google Keep*, *Save to Google Drive*, *One-Click Full-Page*, *Screenshot*, *Google Translate*, *Google Calendar Small PDF*, *Bitmoji*, and *Giphy*.

Content Curation

With all the links, information, and resources out there, you need a place to curate the content. Content curation is the process of gathering information relevant to a particular topic or area of interest, often with the intention of organizing and sharing the content. Other names include social bookmarking or tagging. It helps if you want to access something for further reference, or if you want to share resources with your audiences, colleagues, and other interested stakeholders.

Wakelet is a content-curation platform where teachers and students can save links, social media posts, videos, and images as items for later organization into private or public collections. Users can add notes to each item in order to tell a story, ask questions, or give directions. *Pinterest* is a virtual pin board where you can pin images from various sites, link to the source, and organize by their topic.

"Wakelet allows you to not only curate resources for yourself, but to curate resources for different stakeholders," Amanda Jones, teacher librarian at Live Oak Middle School

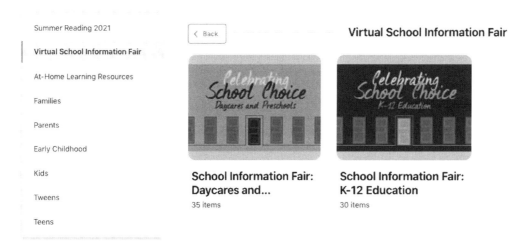

Figure 8.1. Sample Wakelet. *Arlington Heights Memorial Library*

in Denham Springs, Louisiana, said. "Those resources can be PDFs, websites, pictures, videos, tweets, etc. You can then embed a Wakelet resource board into your website or send it out via a link."

Collaboration Tools

Collaboration tools provide ways for students, teams, coworkers, and project groups to work together and communicate remotely. *Padlet* is a compact wall layout with templates, backgrounds, and sticky notes. There is a password protection option and the walls work to share suggestions, book choices, or other ideas. *Flipgrid* is a free video discussion platform where users can join groups and record short video responses to questions using video technology. It also features integrations with several other applications.

Form Builders

A form builder is a way to create web forms where people can input personal information, answer questions, or participate in activities. Many sites have built-in form functions. *Google Forms* is a versatile product that's part of the web-based suite and used for RSVPs,

Figure 8.2. Google Form digital escape room. *Naperville Public Library*

digital escape rooms, quizzes, and beyond. *Typeform* is a web building tool, with templates, predefined questions, and advanced customization.

"I enjoy using Google Forms the most for online instruction," Jones said. "I am able to embed videos, pictures, quizzes, and more and link them to our library's website."

Games

A key theme in this guide is that online programs are much more successful with interaction. Digital games take interaction to a new level. Many resources allow you to input your own data to make games, while other popular classic games have web versions that can be a good break during a session. On *Deck Toys* you make activities on a game board complete obstacles to reach a final destination. *Flippity* is a top resource for Google Sheets to create matching, scavenger hunts, board games, puzzles, and more. In August of 2021 Flippity was experiencing problems with Google Security upgrades and working to return to full functionality.[2]

There are several fun quiz apps online including *Socrative*, *Kahoot*, and *Quizizz*. They work well in a classroom or social nature.

Graphics

Online graphic design makes content user-friendly and engaging. An infographic uses pictures and words to show information and make it more understandable. Infographics embed onto screens or web pages and promote discussion.

Canva is a free web and phone infographic creator. It requires an account and has free and premium options, with a vast array of templates, images, and ability to do things on your own. It also has a nonprofit and classroom version, which your organization may qualify for. *Piktochart* is a free infographic creator on the web or an app that requires an account and has a variety of icons and templates. It requires an account and has a variety of icons and templates.

Green-Screen Apps

Green screens allow you to make your background disappear and transfer elsewhere. They can be helpful for adding dimension to a video, or concealing your location for privacy. When choosing a background, try to find one that's not too busy or visually distracting. A professional green screen is the best, but it's not always a practical choice.

A problem I commonly have with green screens, is finding a blank wall that does not wash me out. Sometimes, it helps to drape a green- or blue-colored blanket over a couch or wall. A green tablecloth, green bulletin board, or wrinkle-free bed sheet is another idea. It's also important to not wear a shirt the same color as the backdrop or your body will blend right in. Many videorecording softwares like Zoom have built-in green screens.

Green Screen by *Do Ink* is easy to use for green-screen videos—you can add your own background or video. *TouchCast Studio* is a free iPad app that has premade backgrounds, or you can insert your own. *Green Screen Pro* is an app only available for Mac iOS that allows you to upload and add a background image.

Just for Fun

Some apps and resources might not have a ton of educational purpose, but adding fun and creativity to a situation serves an important purpose. *Zoom Call Soundboard* is basically a digital sound machine that plays fun audio snippets and is available on apps other than Zoom. *Confetti* is a chrome extension that rains confetti all over your screen if you are screen sharing. The *Uhmmm* app automatically plays elevator music when online meetings go silent.

Meme Makers

A meme is typically humorous with a ridiculous photo paired with a clever caption. Creating your own memes can help create a community and levity. *ImgFlip* is one of the most-used meme creators for producing popular memes like Grumpy Cat, the Philosoraptor, and the fist-pumping baby. You can also upload your own photo to create a meme. *Photoshop Mix* is a free meme generator for iPhone and Android that has advanced features including the ability to layer up to ten items.

Photo Editors

Photo editors change, enhance, and combine photos. These editors make web resources more visually based, which can increase accessibility. *PicCollage* is a web platform that's available as a phone app. It requires an account and creates collages where you can add text and upload to media. *Flipsnack* is a web browser app that transforms PDF files into a digital flipbook. It requires an account and is free to use, but you need a premium account to download a flipbook. These books can showcase a variety of images and integrate with social media.

Podcasts

A podcast is a digital audio file made available online for downloading to a computer or mobile device. It is typically available as a series and new installments are sent automatically to subscribers. They are easy to use and many have technology tricks and recommendations. *Voice Memo* software on phones is the cheapest and easiest way to record audio. The recording quality is not a high level. *SoundCloud* is a free audio recorder available as a desktop app or on iPhone and Android. You can record and save podcast episodes. *Anchor. fm* is a popular podcast recording system because it's a community site with thousands of podcasts. You do not need to find a hosting site or create your own RSS feed. Stations have URLs. Audio clips remain in the cloud for twenty-four hours unless published. *Audacity* is a high-quality software if you want more control of editing and saving of your podcast. *Podcastic* and *Impatica* are also strong podcasting tools.

Polls and Surveys

Polls are the process of voting for something and are an easy way to gain audience participation and feedback. Many platforms have built-in polling systems, but there are also creative add-ons. Surveys and polls are an easy way to gain immediate feedback, sort people into ideas, or break the ice. A survey allows for multiple questions while a poll usually only has one question.

Mentimeter is an online presentation software that allows you to poll people live and receive results in real time, and can be converted to charts, word clouds, and other visualizations. Mentioned above, *Google Forms* is popular for polls where you can compile results into a spreadsheet. *Poll Everywhere* offers free educational results available live and then integrated into a presentation. Several poll types are available, including multiple choice, word cloud, question and answer, rank order, clickable image, survey, and open-ended. Responses are anonymous and limited to forty per poll. *SurveyMonkey* is a commonly used resource that links to a Google or Facebook account and applies to various categories. It is helpful for more detailed surveys and because many users have familiarity with it.

Presentations

The presentation is the basis and core of any session. It is accessible and helpful to have slides to download after a session, or something visual for attendees to follow along with. *Google Slides* is a commonly used, shareable, and editable resource, but there are other pre-made options. *Pear Deck* is a Google Slide add-on that allows you to add interactive questions and live participation. There are free and paid accounts—the paid account allows for live responses. *Prezi* is an interactive video presentation tool that makes use of one large canvas. Prezi allows viewers to pan and zoom to various parts of the canvas and emphasize ideas presented there. *SlidesCarnival* is my all-time favorite source for free slide templates with no registration and no download limits.

QR Codes

QR stands for quick response. QR codes are 2D barcodes that can store and digitally present more data than standard barcodes. You can point a smartphone camera at a QR code to scan it, or go through a website if you don't have a mobile device. It makes it easier for non–English speakers to access resources and use fewer physical resources. QR codes are either static or dynamic. Static codes simply encode the information at one time, while dynamic codes redirect to a website, and the redirection URL can change. You can create your own QR code with *Chrome Extension*, which generates a QR code from a single page, or *QR Stuff*, where you can create QR codes for more than twenty data types and smartphones.

Reference Materials

Many libraries provide a collection of electronic resources available to students, faculty, and staff. The electronic collections include databases, library catalogs, online journals, and Internet resources. Popular electronic databases are *ERIC Database* (via EBSCO-host), which has a full-text database of education research and information. *JSTOR* provides access to academic journals and books covering a wide range of disciplines and includes limited primary source collections. *Zotero* is a free and open-source reference management software that manages bibliographic data and related research materials.

Screencast

A screencast is a video recording of data displayed on a screen with accompanying audio. It is helpful in technology tutorials, and a viewer can play it many times to increase understanding. Screencasting is a quick, easy, and effective way of sharing knowledge. *Camtasia* is an all-in-one screen recorder and video editor with standard recording options and exclusive enhancing features. It is user-friendly but has a high learning curve. *OBS Studio* is an open-source software that has advanced recording and livestreaming possibilities. It provides a fast way to screen-capture videos with simple visual effects. The *Flipgrid Shorts* camera can integrate with several systems and allows you to record your screen and combine screen and video recordings. *Screencastify* is a screen recorder on Google Chrome that easily integrates with other Google applications.

Frank Skornia, digital librarian in Information and Adult Services at the Ferguson Library in Stamford, Connecticut, wholeheartedly recommends OBS Studio. "I would absolutely recommend OBS Studio," Skornia said. "Its open-source flexibility and reliability make it one of the most useful tools available for doing anything video related on the computer. It is essential if you are looking at livestream or teaching through a teleconferencing platform—fairly recent updates allow you to set OBS Studio's output

---

TEXTBOX 8.1

Leah Holloway, public relations assistant at Augusta-Richmond County Public Library System in Augusta, Georgia, shares her experiences with library programs on various social platforms.

"The platforms we use for online instruction are Facebook, YouTube, Instagram, TikTok, and Twitter. YouTube is my favorite platform for long-form webinars, programming, or presentations. Facebook follows close behind because we see more engagement on this platform. Livestreamed events through both media have made us more visible to current and potential patrons. Instagram, Twitter, and TikTok are limited with time. We use those platforms from time to time for quick tutorials or promoting programs.

"My favorite program was our Virtual Appleby Concert Series. We hold this event every year, and it is usually in the garden of our Appleby Branch Library. We had to cancel the event in 2020 due to COVID. We worked hard this year to ensure the event would happen virtually. We hired three local artists to participate and streamed the event through our Facebook and YouTube channels. We also hired two audio engineers (whom we hire every year) to ensure sound quality was the best. Patron participation ebbed and flowed. However, in this crisis, I think it was necessary to keep our name out there. I believe that even for those who just saw our programs come across their feed. That's really how social media works. You will have patrons, current or potential, in and out from viewing the event live. The nice thing is that they can watch the performance later if they can't catch it live.

"Our biggest challenge was viewer engagement on our social platforms because we were competing with everything else on Facebook and YouTube Live for views. We could not control how many people saw our events or programming.

"A streaming software can open the doors to potential patrons showing interest in your library. Restream.io is a software that streams our live programming to YouTube and Facebook simultaneously. This software has helped us showcase our library programs and events synchronously while practicing social distancing in our community. Restream has thirty streaming locations available on its platform. Your library may find a new area for market-specific programs."

as a 'virtual camera,' which gives you access to its full range of scenes and transitions on almost any platform. It is also an inexpensive way to do good-quality video recordings on your computer without having to pay for other screencasting software."

Social Networking and Media

Social networking and media sites connect users and can be helpful to link to various people and followers. *Social networking* is the use of dedicated websites and applications to interact with other users, and *social media* consists of the websites and applications that enable users to take part in social networking. They both generate ideas for research, especially for current and pop-culture topics. The sites usually require a login to view content. Linking and reposting is the norm over downloading and repurposing.

Using many social-networking tools can help promote and share content to various demographics. Using the same social media name for multiple networking sites makes you or your organization easier to find. *Facebook*, one of the largest social-networking sites, provides livestreaming, individual pages, or groups for classes or organizations. *Twitter*, a microblogging platform limited to posts (tweets) of 280 characters, exists to share content and start conversations. *Tumblr* is a microblogging platform with short snippets of information. *Instagram* is popular for photo sharing and short stories to show off in-the-moment happenings. *Goodreads* is a social-networking site for books, used by many librarians with different bookshelves. *TikTok* is a short-form video-sharing application with fifteen-second videos on any topic.

Student Portfolios

In virtual classrooms students need a place to display their work. Private class options are helpful, but there are fun options to share work with a larger voice. *Seesaw* has multimodal tools that allow students to easily capture and share what they know. *Artsonia* is a gallery of digital student art portfolios for grades K–12.

Teacher Tools

School librarians and teachers can find many beneficial tools, and there are many specific networks out there for school librarians. The paid version of *EasyBib* offers a plagiarism check, and the free version creates citations in all major styles. *Clever* is a single sign-on application for education where you can put authenticated links in one place for ease of access and use. *Parlay* is a comprehensive discussion platform with virtual and in-person reactions. Students can split their screens, and they have a toolbar where they can "tap in" to build on an idea, ask a question, challenge a thought, or introduce a new concept. Attendees can tap in and out when finished and instructors can receive a summary of the action at the end.

Video Formatting and Resources

There are countless resources for video recording, editing, formatting, and curating. Chapter 6, "Choosing a Platform," dives deeper into more video resources. *Edpuzzle* creates interactive video lessons and allows users to embed interactive questions directly into videos, so a video will pause at the question and only restart once answered. This feature is beneficial for training videos. There is a Video Options panel on *Google Slides* that allows you to edit and trim a video to the desired size in Google Slides.

Virtual Reality

Virtual reality (VR) is the use of computer technology to create a simulated environment. A participant most commonly uses a headset to enter a virtual environment. Common VR devices are *HTC Vive*, *Oculus Rift*, and *Google Cardboard*. Many VR headsets have age limitations and disclaimers for motion sickness or headaches. There are many premade VR tours ready to use. Augmented reality (AR) adds digital elements to a live view. Examples are the game Pokémon Go or a Snapchat filter. A mixed reality (MR) experience combines elements of both AR and MR where the elements of real and imagined worlds interact. Extended reality (XR) covers all the above-mentioned technologies.

Google Expeditions is a free program, with expeditions in schools and from locations around the world. These expeditions support group viewings. *Google Street View* has VR trips around the world. These allow people to visit solo destinations. *YouTube* has many VR trips that you can find using the 360-degree filter.

Creating your own virtual reality is an option for a program or course. Smartphone cameras make it easier to create panoramic tours. Apps include *Panaroo*, where a video or photos are stitched into a panorama. *Google VR Tour Creator* allows you to use your own imagery or Google Street imagery to create a tour.

Whiteboard

Digital whiteboards are similar to those in the classroom, a place where people can draw and write notes for all to see. Videoconferencing platforms including *Microsoft Teams* and *Zoom* have whiteboard features in the individual videoconferencing platform that the presenter controls, unless he or she gives others privileges. *Jamboard* is a popular collaborative whiteboard that offers slide annotation, sticky note response templates, and a graffiti wall for ideas. *Whiteboard.fi* is an option to give participants individual whiteboards to work on and share.

Wikis

A wiki is a website with collaborative editing and structured information with a table of contents. It can be ideal for research projects, knowledge bases, and workplace manuals. The most commonly used wiki host is *MediaWiki*, which Wikipedia uses, and other options include *PBworks* (formerly PBwiki), *Wikispaces*, and *Tiki Wiki*.

Word Cloud Systems

A word cloud, or tag cloud, is a visual representation of text. The size or weight of the words depends on how many times a word or phrase appears in a text. Clouds are a visual representation of concepts and compile survey results and thoughts.

Google Docs, *Microsoft Word*, and *Microsoft PowerPoint* all have free word cloud add-ons.

TagCrowd is a web-based application used for free word clouds that are editable, downloadable, and sharable. *Wordclouds.com* works on PC, tablet, or smartphone and is a simple creator with minimal special features.

ⓖ Recommending Resources

As a librarian and instructor, any resource you use in a presentation should be a walking recommendation. Attendees may ask you what you used and for more information on it. That is why it is important to research and understand your resources before using them. Recommending a web resource should follow the same process as recommending a book or other materials, and the librarian should conduct a reference interview to determine the best resource.

When using or referencing a resource in a program, provide links to the external resources and try to provide them in a central point of access, like a handout or a pathfinder.

ⓖ Support Systems and Networks

One of the best aspects of libraries being in so many locations across the country and world is that librarians everywhere are working with your similar mission and goals. Connecting with other librarians can help save a lot of troubleshooting time, create connections in the workforce, and aid in sharing resources.

Erin Weaver, the assistant director of the Bridgeville Public Library in Bridgeville, Pennsylvania, stresses the importance of finding a network. "There's no need to reinvent the wheel," Weaver said. "I recommend looking into library Facebook groups and reaching out to peers. Also, don't worry if you try a new platform and it doesn't get a good response. The important thing is that you tried something new and learned from the experience."

Many digital support systems or professional learning networks (PLNs) exist for online instruction. Look into specific forums for whichever platform you use: listservs, Facebook groups, social media hashtags, and online support centers created by vendors with documentation. Advice from real users is often the most helpful, especially if you are experiencing unusual technical difficulties. Conferences also provide a forum for discussion and talks about lesser-known topics. The Internet is endless, so try to find resources and people you trust and stick with them so that you don't get lost in the World Wide Web.

Facebook groups include:

- Programming Librarian Interest Group on Facebook, which looks at virtual programming specifically for an adult age group.
- Library Think Tank #ALATT, formerly known as ALA Think Tank, is one of the largest social networks of library employees.
- Technology Training and Libraries shares technology and literacy training for staff and the public.
- Elearning in Libraries is a forum about developing online learning for libraries including screencasts, tutorials, videos, and any other format delivered in an online format for library staff or patrons.
- Imagine Your Virtual Story began at the onset of the COVID-19 pandemic for librarians to share virtual programming ideas.

The website www.programminglibrarian.org is managed by the American Library Association Public Programs Office and offers resources, ideas, and professional development opportunities for library professionals who do programming.

On Twitter or Instagram, you can try #hashtagging any resource or technology tool you are looking for information on. Other helpful technology- and library-based hashtags include #edtech, #techtools, #internetlibrarian, and #librarytwitter.

⊚ Key Points

- Find quality technology resources that will supplement and improve your presentation.
- Evaluate a resource force and make sure that it will benefit your presentation and your audience.
- Explore, practice, and test. Try something out (ideally more than once) before using it with the public.
- Find networks and resources you trust to build a community and share ideas.

⊚ Notes

1. Curtis Jay Bonk and Ke Zhang, *Empowering Online Learning: 100+ Activities for Reading, Reflecting, Displaying, and Doing* (San Francisco: Jossey-Bass, 2008).
2. "What's Wrong?" Flippity.net, accessed October 28, 2021, www.flippity.net/WhatsWrong.htm.

Copyright

COPYRIGHT IS A SET OF RIGHTS IN US law that grants ownership to the authors of "original works of authorship," including but not limited to literary, drama, music, art, and audiovisual works. This chapter explains different aspects of copyright; however, it is not official legal advice. Copyright issues have made many headlines in the legal world and many libraries received cease-and-desist letters for infringing on copyright. All the information provided in this chapter is educational. Do not consider this information as legal advice and still do your own research. Any decisions or official information must go through your specific organization.

Copyright law changes the way libraries provide information to their users, and though the First Sale Doctrine allows libraries to lend their items, regulations can get complicated in a digital format. As technology and education evolve, so will emerging challenges with technology, copyright, and original work.

Copyright is very tricky and confusing, and people can get into a great deal of trouble, so it is important to tread carefully. The amount of attention you give to copyright depends on what material you use and how you use it. Specifically, in libraries and educational institutions, broad interpretations exist for fair use. It is always crucial to abide by your institutional policy. All instances are unique and sometimes information is acceptable for use.

Copyright law protects creative work, including but not limited to literary, musical, dramatic, pictorial, graphic, audio, and audiovisual work. Digital items protected under copyright are blogs, web pages, images, and software programs.

There are many misconceptions about digital copyright, including but not limited to: all online works are in the public domain; digital materials without a copyright notice are not under copyright; if a copyright holder does not respond to a media request, then the items are free to use.

Copyright law does not protect one person's ideas or discoveries. This chapter cannot cover every aspect of copyright law, so when in doubt, seek legal counsel. As copyright law gets updated and new cases enter court, keep abreast of the latest information about your specific specialty.

Foundational Questions

When considering copyright, take a moment to consider your organization and your own ethics and policies along with copyright and ethics. Think about your priorities before you use and share online content. Check if you are using the content someone else created and if you are crediting the creator. Think about how the use of this source may impact the creator or owner.

A lot of differing views concerning copyright came into play during COVID-19. What is fair use? What is the difference between in-person and online? It is hard for a society to determine the line, and it's important to establish a line for yourself or your organization and to stick by that standard.

If you follow the rules and keep most of your coursework closed and password protected, then you will hopefully not get into any legal trouble. Rules to follow include: linking whenever possible, providing citations, digitizing media only when other digital versions are not available, and providing access for a limited number of people and a limited duration of time.

Other ideas that can be super-safe for copyright are using your original work (unless published or owned by someone other than yourself), materials in the Creative Commons, or materials that clearly state availability for use, media, or materials that your institution has purchased a license to use, materials in the public domain, and links to cited websites.

History of Copyright

In one of the first acts of the US Congress, a national copyright law passed in 1790.[1] "An act for the encouragement of learning, by securing the copies of maps, charts, and books, to the authors and proprietors of such copies during the time therein mentioned." Copyright law receives edits and revisions with time to modify the length of copyright, create categories, and modify procedures for acquiring copyright. The current copyright law in the United States, along with subsequent amendments, is the Copyright Act of 1976.

There were several additional amendments for copyright that make resources more available in educational institutions and after a prolonged time period. These laws are helpful in making more information available to use.

The duration of copyright is somewhat complicated and depends on a work's creation date.[2] For works created on January 1, 1978, or later, the copyright lasts for the life of the longest living author plus 70 years, and for works for hire and anonymous or pseudonymous works, 95 years from publication or 120 years from creation, whichever comes first. For works created and published or registered before January 1, 1978:

1. First term of 28 years from the date published with a copyright notice or registered in unpublished form.
2. During the last 28 years, copyright is eligible for renewal. Automatic renewal as effective between January 1, 1964, and December 31, 1977.
3. If copyright was in effect on January 1, 1978, the renewal term was extended from 28 to 47 years for pre-1978 copyrights restored under the Uruguay Round Agreements Acts (URAA) for a total protection of 75 years.

ⓖ Expanded Legislation

Libraries and educational institutions often use information for education and sharing. Legislation exists to make the dissemination easier for such purposes, although it has very specific criteria.

Fair Use

Fair use is a term used in libraries to "work around" copyright law in the United States. It is a doctrine of US law that allows for limited use of copyrighted material without needing to seek permission from the owner.

The four main factors for fair use are:

1. The purpose and character of the use, including whether such use is of a commercial nature or is for nonprofit educational purposes.
2. The nature of the copyrighted work.
3. The quantity and substance of the portion used in relation to the copyrighted work as a whole.
4. The effect of the usage on the potential market for or value of the copyrighted work.

Courts make legal decisions for fair use on a case-by-case basis. Information used and the audience can be a big part of the determination. Many publishers allow librarians or instructors to read full books on unlisted channels or in a live session. During the onset of COVID-19, many viewed fair use liberally due to extreme situations. As the pandemic moved on, publishers and organizations began to create specific permissions for their works.

Public Domain

Public domain applies to work where copyright does not apply because the copyright is expired, forfeited, waived, or inapplicable. In the United States, every book published prior to 1926 is in the public domain, and American copyrights last for ninety-five years for books originally published between 1925 and 1978.[3]

TEACH Act of 2002

The Technology, Education, and Copyright Harmonization (TEACH) Act of 2002 provides special guidance for academic institutions.[4] Under the TEACH Act, instructors may use a range of works in distance-learning environments, students may participate in distance-learning sessions from virtually any location, and participants receive more freedom with storing, copying, and digitizing materials. Under this act, one can download online images for teaching without prior permission if done in a way that does not allow attendees to copy the images. The same applies to audio and video, but there are length limitations: videos of up to three minutes or 10 percent (whichever is shorter), music to 10 percent of the composition with a limit of thirty seconds. This act allows you to post materials online that exist on a physical display in an educational institution. The TEACH Act requires you to add a legal notice that online materials "may" be subject to copyright protection.[5]

The specific criteria for copyrighted materials in distance education under the TEACH Act are:

- The institution must be an accredited, nonprofit educational institution.
- The materials must be part of a planned instructional event.
- The use must be limited to a specific number of students enrolled in a specific class.
- The use must either be for "live" or asynchronous class sessions. The content cannot be recorded.

Digital Millennium Copyright Act of 1998 (DMCA)

An amendment to the Copyright Act of 1976 that made it possible for the United States to join two World Intellectual Property Organization (WIPO) treaties concluded in Geneva in December 1996. The amendment updated the copyright law to deal with new technology. This act prohibits the circumvention of technical copyright protection measures. Two exemptions allow nonprofit libraries, archives, or educational institutions to circumvent copyright systems to determine if they wish to acquire a copy and to make fair use of a lawfully acquired work. Provisions also exist with distance learning, library preservation, and liability of online service providers.

⑥ Publisher Permissions

Many organizations like to stick to the conservative side and ask for permission to use resources. One of the most frequent questions to come up during COVID-19 was reading and recording picture books and chapter books online. Many publishers issued blanket permissions for a given amount of time. A blog post from the ALA Programming Office saying that books qualified under fair use also circulated widely.[6] These permissions typically have various caveats, like naming the publisher and author, posting in a closed medium, and taking the video down after a predetermined length of time. These restrictions are legal as a copyright holder sets limits on who may use the materials, for how long, and in which ways. Authors reading their own work need to abide by these rules. Oftentimes, people treat a live digital program the same as an in-person program, while with recorded programs it can be imperative to follow the guidelines. When in doubt, check with your organization and the owner of the work. It is ideal for organizations to create a set policy for how staff members handle fair use and permissions. Also, create a plan for what to do when temporary permissions expire.

To request individual permission, contact the copyright holder, which is often the publisher. Many publishers have sites stating their copyright permissions policy and offering forms for people to fill out. When contacting a copyright holder for permission to read a book during story time, include:

- Your name, title, institution, and type of institution.
- Your contact information: email address, phone number, and physical address.
- Your method of sharing the book (YouTube, Class Dojo, Canvas, Zoom, etc.).
- Describe how you will store the information.
- The book titles and ISBNs that you plan on reading.
- Ask if more information is needed and thank the publisher for considering the request.

Figure 9.1 shows a sample email to a publisher asking for permissions to read a book in story time.

Not everyone agrees with the long legal process of copyright, especially depending on the use. There are creators who want to share their creativity and knowledge. That's where open copyright licenses come into play.

Creative Commons

Creative Commons is a global nonprofit organization that enables sharing and reuse of resources with international licenses. Creative Commons' license requires users to provide attribution to the creator. The most basic license is the BY license, which requires users to provide attribution to the creator when using and sharing material. Additional levels include NonCommerical (NC), which bans commercial use of material; NoDerivatives

---

Emily Mroczek <emilyrmroczek@gmail.com>   1:40 PM (1 minute ago)   ↩ ⋮

to publisher ▾

To Whom It May Concern,

My name is Emily Mroczek and I am a freelance children's librarian for the public library in Woodridge, IL. I am hoping to read your book "Online Instructing," by Emily Mroczek, ISBN 8754829485in a Zoom storytime on Monday Oct. 24 2021 at 10:30 am.The storytime will be recorded for our viewers and shared on Youtube.

Please let me know if any further information is required and thank you for considering my request.

Emily Mroczek
Freelance Librarian
888 Instruction St.
555-555-5555

Figure 9.1.   Sample copyright request email. *Emily Mroczek*

(ND), which does not allow creating and sharing adaptations of materials; and ShareA-like (SA), which places adapted material under the same license. Creative Commons is useful for publicly accessible online courses, MOOCs (Massive Open Online Courses), and social media.

Open Educational Resources and Open Access Materials

Open educational resources (OER) and open-access materials have many instructional resources that are free to use. Typically, these resources allow sharing and re-sharing by anyone. The "5 R" permissions of OER allow you to take your usage to the next level and modify for your individual needs. They are: retain, reuse, revise, reorder, and redistribute, which ultimately allow users to own, edit, and share content as desired. The OER Commons provide resources for instructors to find quality material for their needs.

⑥ Image Resources

Two-dimensional images (photographs) are subject to copyright law. As images exist in most web instruction, it is important to find open-source images or ones you have permission to use. There are a large number of image-sharing sites, where members generate content, and the information accompanying images and rights over content varies depending on the contributors.

Creative Commons: One of the largest image-sharing sites with strong content in photography, travel, and architecture.

Flickr's the Commons: A subset of Flickr images, where content is from cultural institutions around the world and has historical, public domain, and materials with no known copyright.

Wikimedia Commons: Includes images contributed by the public, which contain public domain, open, and Creative Commons images.

Several US government agencies make images available to the public through the agencies' websites. Created for documentary, educational, informational, or communication purposes, many of these images are public and free for use. Look for rights statements and disclaimers about copyright status.

Several stock-image websites include photographs taken by professional or contributing individuals. Many sites have a fee to access and use images, while others have specific policies to embed an image with a link back to their site. If you use *Google Images*, you can do an advanced image search and under Usage Rights, click Labeled for Reuse filter for Free to Use or Share.

Getty Images has many images with code included to embed directly into blogs and websites. The Getty Open Content Program specifically has images that are free to use.

ACRL's Image Resources Interest Group hosts a *Digital Images Collections Guide* on ALA Connect for image resources organized by subject.

The Noun Project has icons, symbols, and graphics available for download if you create an account.

Library Databases and Discovery systems provide access to many images. Specific permissions vary depending on the database, with many prohibiting use on the open web but allowing it in closed presentations with a limited audience. Large library galleries include:

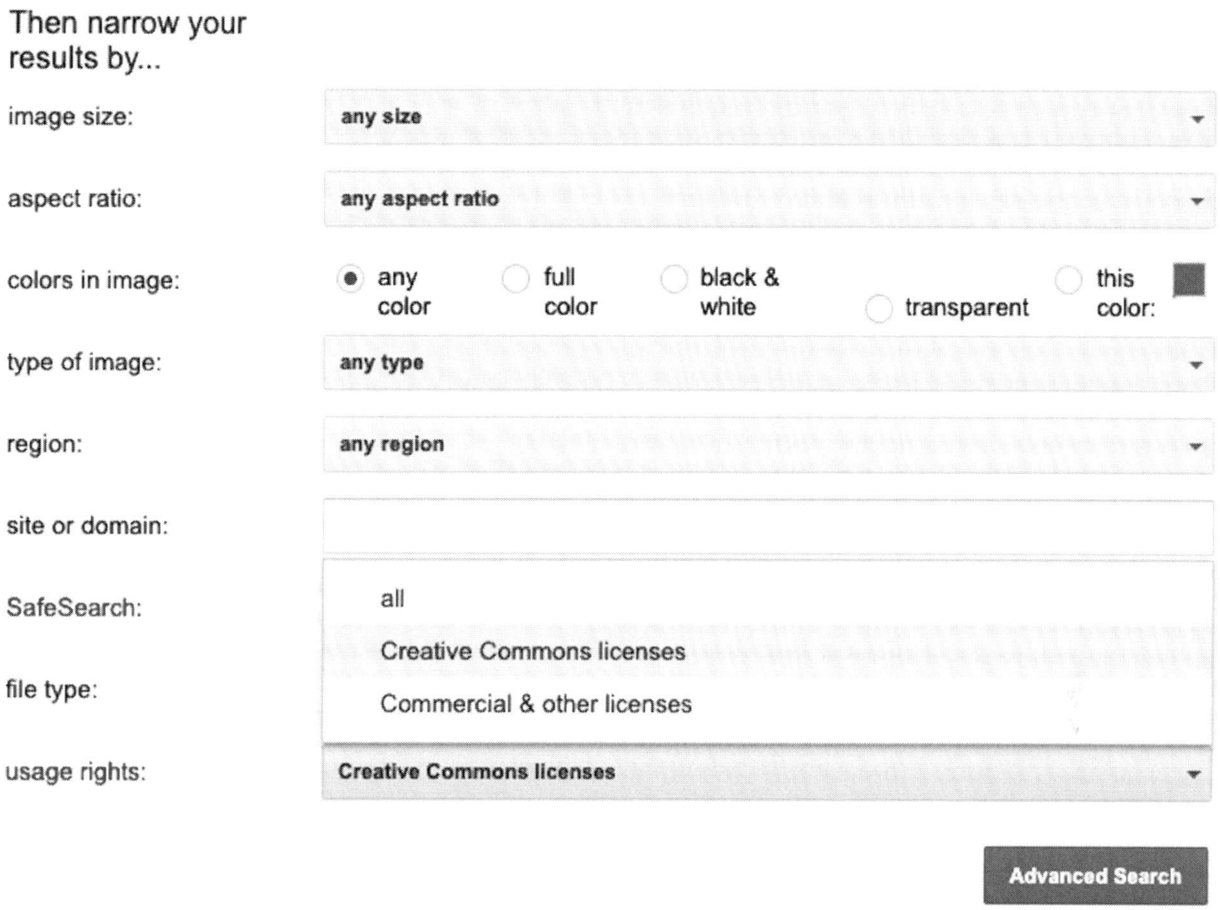

Then narrow your results by...

image size: | any size ▾

aspect ratio: | any aspect ratio ▾

colors in image: | ● any color ○ full color ○ black & white ○ transparent ○ this color: ■

type of image: | any type ▾

region: | any region ▾

site or domain: |

SafeSearch: | all

file type: | Creative Commons licenses

 | Commercial & other licenses

usage rights: | **Creative Commons licenses** ▾

Advanced Search

Figure 9.2. Advanced Google Image search. *Google*

- *World Digital Library*, a part of the Library of Congress, which partners with agencies around the world to make multilingual primary-source materials freely available.
- *Digital Public Library of America*, a discovery tool that retrieves materials from library, archive, and museum digital collections.
- *NYPL Digital Gallery* has manuscripts, maps, posters, photographs, and other images from the New York Public Library. Medium-size images are free to download, while larger images have a cost.
- *AP Images* is available through many library systems and includes photographs, audio, and graphics from the Associated Press dating back to the 1800s.
- *Every Stock Photo* is a search engine for free stock photos with license icons that will list permissions.

Music Resources

Section 101 of the copyright law defines sound recordings as works that result from the fixation of a series of musical, spoken, or other sounds. The sounds accompanying a motion picture or other audiovisual work are not included in Section 101. When looking for music to use in a program or video, check for Royalty Free sounds. For story times, songs in the public domain are available.

Copyright laws protect most music on the Internet. Under the Music Modernization Act,[7] *recordings* have federal copyright-like protection. Previously, sound recordings were protected inconsistently by state law and did not enter the public domain. The MMA established a public domain for sound recordings ninety-five years after the first publication, subject to additional time periods.

- For recordings first published before 1923, the additional time period ends on December 31, 2021.
- For recordings first published between 1923 and 1946, the additional time period is five years after the general ninety-five-year term.
- For recordings first published between 1947 and 1956, the additional time period is fifteen years after the general ninety-five-year term.
- For all remaining recordings first fixed prior to February 15, 1972, the additional transition period shall end on February 15, 2067.

If using audio for internal promotions and content, check if your specific purpose works under the Fair Use Act. *Freeplay Music* allows you to search for music by style and mood. Files save as an MP3. *Getty Free Music* hosts royalty-free music and audio clips, with usage rights that are easy to understand. *SoundCloud* has a specific section for royalty-free music with loops in a wide genre and style and licensing details listed. The *Public Domain Information Project* was organized in 1986 to provide information about public domain music including public domain music titles, PD sheet music reprints, and PD sheet music books.

Frequently Asked Questions

What do I do if I'm not sure about permissions?
The safest answer is to reach out to the creator or publisher of the information. You can find contact information on their web page, and they can grant specific permission.

How do I protect my own work?
Make sure to password-protect your work (one way is through Adobe Acrobat), put your name and information on everything, and clearly state what is free for public use or any individual standards and requests you have.

What is the difference between plagiarism and copyright?
Plagiarism and copyright infringement have many similarities but are two separate concepts. Plagiarism is using another's work without naming the source, while copyright infringement is reproducing, modifying, performing, or displaying a work without receiving explicit permission.

How do I know if something is in the public domain?
In the United States, works published before 1923 are generally in the public domain. Audio recordings from before February 15, 1972, are an exception and protected by state law. In other countries, national laws and the definition of public domain apply within those borders.

What happens if I receive a cease-and-desist letter?
It is important to take these letters seriously and report them to your supervisor or organization's legal counsel. From there, you can decide the next steps, which could include complying with the letter's demands or taking an alternative form of action. The letter is not legally binding, but serves as a warning and is a potential precursor to a lawsuit.

What isn't protected by copyright?
Copyright law in the United States does not cover "any idea, procedure, process, system, method of operation, concept, principle, or discovery." It also does not protect works prepared by an officer or an employee of the US government as a part of that person's official duties.

What if I really want to use something but don't have permission?
One can contact the copyright holder and ask for permission. The copyright holder might grant permission, deny permission, or ask for a possibly substantial fee. Securing permissions can be a long and costly process, but it is manageable if it's something that can really influence your content.

What if something is from another country and there are different laws?
A general rule is to go with the stricter copyright laws to avoid any issues.

Key Terms

Terms to know when learning about copyright include:

All rights reserved: Formerly a required phrase in copyright notice under the Buenos Aires convention. The phrase is no longer required as of March 1, 1989.

Best practice codes: Documents created for individual communities to help users make informed decisions about copyright and fair use.

Cease-and-desist order: A cease-and-desist letter is a cautionary notice detailing the sender's complaint of an alleged wrongdoing and threatening legal action if the offending activity continues.

Common law copyright: An author's right to his or her work that is believed to have existed before a written statute existed.

Copyright: The bundle of rights that belong to a copyright holder to control how works are used by others.

Copyright Act of 1976: The current copyright law in the United States including subsequent amendments. Effective January 1, 1978.

Copyright owner: The owner of the particular right in copyright.

Copyright term: The amount of time a work is covered by copyright due to copyright law.

De minimis rule: An apparent infringement where the amount is so insignificant that it does not rise to the level of infringement.

Digital Performance Right in Sound Recordings Act of 1995 (DPRA): Amendment to the Copyright Act of 1976 that granted public performance rights to copyright holders of sound recordings.

Display: To show a copy of a work, either directly or by means of a film, slide, television image, or any other device or process or, in the case of a motion picture or other audiovisual work, to show individual images inconsequentially.

Educational use: Use in educational contexts that directly relates to educational pursuits.

Fair use: A copyright law provision that allows for use in specific circumstances such as criticism, comment, scholarship, or research.

First-sale doctrine: The first-sale doctrine is an American legal concept that limits the rights of an intellectual property owner to control resale of products embodying its intellectual property.

Fixation of a work: A work consisting of sounds, or images, is fixed if a fixation of the work is being made simultaneously with its transmission.

Infringement: Unauthorized, unexempted use of a work by one other than the copyright holder.

Intellectual property: Products and results of a person's creative or intellectual work.

License agreement: An agreement between content providers or users to determine how the content can be accessed and used.

Open access (OA): Content made freely available online without restrictions on access or use.

Performance: To perform a work means to recite, render, play, dance, or act it directly or by means of any device or process or, in the case of the motion picture or other audiovisual works, to show its images in any sequence.

Public domain: Works not covered by copyright because the copyright term has expired.

Terms of use: Descriptions of how specific databases, resources, or images in them can be used.

Transformative use: A consideration made to evaluate fair use that refers to changes of original work.

Copyright Resources

Several organizations exist to help librarians navigate copyrights and can help answer questions as one works with online teaching.

The US Copyright Office, a department of the Library of Congress: This office administers the 1976 Copyright Act and related laws. The Registrar of Copyrights advises Congress on national and international copyright measures. Their website has detailed policy explanations, frequently asked questions, and resources for registration.

The Copyright Advisory Network—ALA OITP: The Copyright Advisory Network through the American Library Association Office for Information Technology Policy (ALA OITP) works to help librarians respond to copyright law and become more knowledgeable so librarians can serve as advisors to the public on copyright. The network consists of an open forum for advice from copyright scholars, Creative Commons tools explaining copyright, and links to web resources. Tools include the Copyright Genie, the Fair Use Evaluator, and the Public Domain Slider. These tools are embeddable into a web page. The advice can be very helpful, but it is not official legal advice.

The Copyright Information Center at Cornell University: Cornell's website includes facts on copyright policy, clearance service, training, and tutorials. They also have a very detailed chart that can be a quick reference for determining if a work is in the public domain.

The Library Copyright Alliance is comprised of the American Library Association (ALA), the Association of College and Research Libraries (ACRL), and the Association of Research Libraries (ARL). The organizations work together to address copyright issues in libraries and to create a unified voice for libraries responding to national and international copyright law.

EIFL Handbook on Copyright and Related Issues for Libraries: This practical guide by Electronic Information for Libraries (EIFL) addresses policy aspects and legal issues.

For all the items under copyright, there are items that cannot be placed under copyright. These include names, ideas, works by the US federal government, works not in a tangible form of expression, and authorship. As stated, this chapter is by no means an all-inclusive look at copyrights. Familiarize yourself with the laws that concern you and keep up with changes in copyright law.

⊚ Key Points

- Familiarize yourself with copyright legislation.
- There are many royalty-free resources available to use in presentations.
- Make sure you are following your organization's copyright policies.
- This section is not official legal advice, and when it doubt, consult a lawyer.

⊚ Further Reading

Bielefield, Arlene, and Lawrence Cheeseman. *Technology and Copyright Law: A Guidebook for the Library, Research, and Teaching Professions.* New York: Neal-Schuman Publishers, 2007.
Creative Commons for Educators and Librarians. Chicago: ALA Editions, 2020.
Ellis, Erin L., and Kevin Lindsay Smith. *Coaching Copyright.* Chicago: ALA Editions, 2020.

⊚ Notes

1. "Copyright Act of 1790: U.S. Copyright Office," accessed September 20, 2021. https://copyright.gov/about/1790-copyright-act.html.

2. "Circular 15A Duration of Copyright," Copyright, accessed October 2, 2021, www.copyright.gov/circs/circ15a.pdf.

3. "Copyright Term and the Public Domain in the United States," Copyright Information Center (Cornell), accessed October 2, 2021, https://copyright.cornell.edu/publicdomain.

4. "The TEACH Act," accessed October 2, 2021, www.copyright.com/wp-content/uploads/2015/04/CR-Teach-Act.pdf.

5. Ewagner, "Copyright: Distance Education and the TEACH Act," Advocacy, Legislation & Issues (American Library Association, March 10, 2019), www.ala.org/advocacy/copyright/teachact/distanceeducation.

6. Sarah Ostman, "Online Story Time & Coronavirus: It's Fair Use, Folks," Programming Librarian (ALA Public Programs Office, April 30, 2020), https://programminglibrarian.org/articles/online-story-time-coronavirus-it%E2%80%99s-fair-use-folks.

7. U.S. Copyright Office, "The Music Modernization Act," accessed October 15, 2021, www.copyright.gov/music-modernization/.

Digital Accessibility

ACCESSIBILITY IS ENSURING WEBSITES, resources, and files are available to and usable by as many people as possible. Most often accessibility applies to people with disabilities, but it also includes users with limited connection reliability and lack of access to devices.

Accessibility commonly covers physical spaces, but it also applies digitally. Librarians have a special responsibility to work hard on behalf of stakeholders who face extra difficulties for everything from physical to web access. When planning instruction, keep accessibility in mind for all aspects of programming. Information and communication technologies need to be accessible to all users, whether they have a disability or not.

At first glance, digital programming provides increased accessibility. It eliminates many physical boundaries of attending an event. Attendees can to control volume, pause programs, and watch something multiple times. Many aspects of online programming can be more accessible for those with disabilities, however, it is important to look at a program as a whole to determine tools and fixes to make a program accessible to those with varying disabilities. Some common disabilities that may affect a user's web experience are:

- Visual: blindness or low vision, color blindness, photosensitivity, or tracking difficulties
- Auditory: deaf or hard of hearing
- Mobility: physical disabilities that can affect range of motion or fine motor disabilities
- Cognitive or learning disabilities: autism, dyslexia, or ADD

Federal and state laws dictate accessibility requirements and traditionally participants need to reach out in advance for additional support. Having accessible options readily available can increase the attendance and comfort of attendees.

Many web resources are constantly updating their programs to become more accessible. Throughout 2021, Zoom offered automatic transcription and captioning, although they still recommended having a professional.

Carrie Banks, supervising librarian for Inclusive Services at the Brooklyn Public Library in New York, especially appreciates the ability to pin a specific presenter, for example, an ASL interpreter.

Accessibility traditionally covers disabilities, though we will also cover ways to help people with difficulties accessing the Internet or computers.

"With so many people with disabilities living in poverty and in under-resourced neighborhoods, the phone-in option is critical, and we use it for all of our meetings," Banks said.

Legislation for Disabilities and Accessibility

It is easy to forget to comply with standards for programming and disabilities in a digital format, but the rules still apply and it is crucial to keep accessibility standards when planning programming. The Americans with Disabilities Act of 1990 prohibits discrimination on the basis of disability by public entities. The Family Education Rights and Privacy Act (FERPA) protects individuals' privacy. This law marks information specific to a disability confidential and shared only with faculty and staff involved in the development and implementation of the accommodation plan. For schools specifically, Section 504 of the Rehabilitation Act of 1973 prohibits discrimination on the basis of disability by schools receiving federal funds. The Individuals with Disabilities Act (IDEA) requires public schools to provide all eligible children with disabilities a free and appropriate education. In schools a 504 plan (similar to an IEP but larger and for a broader age group) is a blueprint for how a school will support a student with a disability and remove learning barriers.

In addition to disability legislation, there are guidelines for accessibility, many specifically for the web. Section 508 of the Information Technology Accessibility Standards is the federal law that mandates federally funded organizations to provide employees and members of the public with information comparable for employees with and without disabilities. The Web Content Accessibility Guidelines (WCAG) are guidelines for creating web content that is accessible for people with a wide range of disabilities including blindness/low vision, hearing loss, learning disabilities, cognitive limitations, speech disability, photosensitivity, and combinations of these conditions. The Four Principles of Accessibility, also known as POUR (perceivable, operable, understandable, and robust),[1] are a focus point for the WCAG. The World Wide Web Consortium (W3C) is an international organization where contributors work together to develop guidelines for the web.

It is a legal requirement to provide additional accommodations for people with disabilities when asked. Some potential accommodations are live captioning, American Sign Language (ASL) interpretation, and documents in accessible formats.

The Assistive Technology Act of 1998, amended in 2004, focused on improving access to assistive technology devices for people with disabilities. The 2004 changes allow

---

TEXTBOX 10.1

Four Principles of Accessibility (POUR)

- Perceivable: Information and user interface components must be presentable to users in ways they can perceive (it cannot be invisible to all their senses).
- Operable: User interface components and navigation must be operable. (The interface cannot require interaction that a user cannot perform.)
- Understandable: Information and the operation of user interface must be understandable to all users.
- Robust: Content must be robust enough that it can be interpreted reliably by a wide variety of user agents, including assistive technologies (as technologies evolve, the content should remain accessible).

---

the Secretary of Education to make assistive technology grants to states to maintain statewide programs and statewide activities.[2]

Examples of Accessibility

Accessibility on the web starts with having a comfortable environment for varying learners.[3] As mentioned in previous chapters, basic accessibility fixes include a plain background and focused lighting to reduce sensory distractions. "I advise against virtual backgrounds: It can be difficult for neuro-divergent and neuro-diverse people to process speakers fading in and out," Banks said.

When possible, live captioning is helpful, along with allowing users to pause videos and to control audio. Recording a live session can aid learners who want to rewatch for information they may have missed.

Several livestreaming services offer included live captioning options, which can vary in quality. Better-quality video live-captioning services may be necessary due to specific needs. Live-captioning services are also helpful for beginning readers, foreign language speakers, and English as Second Language learners.

"Turn on and use live captioning," Meghan Kowalski, outreach and reference librarian at the University of the District of Columbia, said. "It's not perfect, but it's better than nothing."

The Described and Captioned Media Program (DCMP) notes that captions should be:[4]

- Synchronized and appear at about the same time as audio delivery
- Equivalent and equal in content to that of the audio, including speaker identification and sound effects.
- Accessible and readily available to those who need or want them.

Captions may be closed or open. Closed captioning can be turned on or off, whereas open captions are added to the video file and cannot be turned off. Closed captioning places the responsibility of turning captions on or off with the viewer. Open captions are distracting for some viewers. Automated captioning is helpful but does not produce the quality the DCMP suggests. DCMP standards are easier to comply with in recorded video captions than live videos.

Transcripts for all audio files can be beneficial for those with hearing loss or those whose first language is not English. In addition to transcripts, auditory descriptions and captions can aid those who are deaf or hard of hearing in understanding what is happening. Descriptions are also important for content that relies on color to convey information for colorblind learners. For those who cannot use computers, there can be a telephone option for live programming.

Documents and resources should showcase a clear and easy-to-read font in neutral colors. A page text needs to contrast against the background and read from a distance. Fonts should be no smaller than 12 points, and in a non-serif font (Arial, Tahoma, or Verdana). Headings can assist reading, and avoid caps lock as it is hard to read.[5] Print digital resources or have an option for a print alternative for those who cannot read on screens. Many programs have options to make font sizes larger or to adjust screen brightness.

Plain language is the clear and effective language your audience can understand the first time they hear or read it. It makes a presenter easier to understand and eases translation by interpreters or live captioners. Tips to use plain language include: Use everyday words and define necessary technical words; omit unneeded words; use short lists, bullets, and additional headings; make use of white space; and keep sentences short. It is helpful to give a preview of major points at the beginning of a presentation, to keep to one topic at a time, and to speak using the active voice. For links, never use "click here," but describe

Table 10.1 Converting Common Phrases into Plain Language

DON'T SAY	INSTEAD SAY
A and/or B	A or B or both
Click here	At this link, find an instruction video
A number of	Some
Designate	Appoint, choose, name
Determine	Decide, figure, find
However	But
Identify	Find, name, show
In a timely manner	On time, promptly
In the amount of	For
In the event of	If
It is essential	Must, need to
It is requested	Please, we request, I request
Said, some, such	The, this, that

what your reader will receive if they click the link. The website plainlanguage.gov offers additional guidance, and table 10.1 shows some common conversions into plain language.

Assistive Technology Devices

Assistive technology includes resources to help people with disabilities access information. Screen readers can help the visually impaired access information through a software program that magnifies text and displays information through voice or refreshable braille displays. These screen readers typically use text-to-speech tools, which need an electronic document, not a scanned copy. If content is not digitally accessible, then the screen reader cannot process much information. To improve screen reader accessibility:[6]

- Use a hierarchy of headings so the screen reader can navigate sections.
- Use heading tags <h1> through <h6> to identify headings. Screen readers do not interpret text that is large, or bold as a heading.
- Don't overuse heading tags. Only use them to introduce following text.
- Lists have separate tags and convey a content structure. Unordered lists <ul> are for content with no order, typically in bullet points. Ordered lists <ol> designate an order, typically numeric. Descriptive lists <dl> apply to pairs like a question-and-answer section or a glossary.
- Describe images with alternative text, explaining the nature and context of the image. This alt text appears in a blank box where the image usually is.
- Forms need to be keyboard accessible with text labels for all controls.

Optical character recognition (OCR) converts images of text into a digital format. Desktop video magnifiers and screen magnifiers are helpful tools that connect to a monitor so the user can magnify, focus, and highlight text among other features. Large print and tactile keyboards work along with wearable devices for visual impairment like OrCam devices, or UV glasses. People with mobility disabilities may use the keyboard instead of the mouse. Individuals should consult their doctors for advice about specialized devices.

Able Player is a free and fully accessible cross-browser HTML5 media player designed by the University of Washington in order to meet the diverse needs and preferences of all users. Able Player is compatible with videos hosted on YouTube or Vimeo.

Many resources and apps exist to assist people with disabilities and help them use screens and computers better. Applications for learners with autism include *Choiceworks Calendar*, an iPhone visual calendar app; and *Verbal Me*, an augmented and alternative communication and choice board application. For vision-related disabilities, *Dragon Dictation* offers voice-to-text features, while *TapTapSee* uses camera and voice-over functions to take a photo and identify it out loud. For the deaf or hard of hearing, *Sorenson BuzzCards* is a flash card application that helps those who cannot sign, and *Signed Stories* provides children's stories performed in American Sign Language.

Running Accessible Programs

Specific platforms should have their accessibility features available on their web page. I highlight specific platforms' accessibility in chapters 4 and 5. Features to look for when deciding on a platform include screen reader support, live automated captioning, usability by ASL interpreters, keyboard shortcuts, and high-contrast mode.

Advertisements and program information should include accessibility information like provided accommodations and a point of contact and deadline for requesting specific accommodations. Many states require this by law, so check with your local agencies. It is key to promote accessible programs to your community so that people know what resources exist. Adding alternate text to images makes your content more accessible and searchable. Connect communities to creators with disabilities by inviting outside virtual program presenters, such as guest speakers.

Organizations should create accessibility policies for programs and inform users what services and resources are available to them. This policy should include information about how to request American Sign Language (ASL) or other modifications to a program.

Other ideas for more accessible programs and websites include simplifying paths to virtual program engagement and reducing links. There should be a clear way for users to access a program. Remember that some attendees need additional processing time: Don't expect everyone to understand everything after hearing it once. Any possible resources (slides, transcripts, videos, images, and chat logs) should be available before or after the program for additional processing time.

Announce all accessibility features at the beginning of a program so they do not go unnoticed. If possible, email out slides before the presentation or provide an alternative link to access visuals. During a presentation, remember not everyone can see slides, so make sure that you explain the content. If you're showing a video, check in advance if a transcript is available. Youdescribe.org is a website where people volunteer to transcribe videos on the Internet and where you can ask a volunteer to transcribe a specific video.

Audio programs, or the option to phone in to a program, provides accessibility for those with limited broadband, a different experience for users, and reduced equipment needs. Delivery options include radio, podcast, and telephone. Some libraries, like the Talking Book Library, use telephone services for those who are unable to access the physical location.

Evaluating Web Accessibility

As stated above, there are many practices that increase access and readability of web pages. Making content engaging and accessible is a balancing act.

Any websites and resources should have an annual review for accessibility, which includes making sure the site, videos, and resources are still up to date. An annual review helps prevent accessibility shortcomings from falling through the cracks.

Questions to ask include: How many clicks does it take to engage with content? Does the product provide keyboard equivalents for all mouse actions? Can the user disable or adjust content? If the user accidentally exits the platform, how easy is it to access again? Can the user start and stop the media? Is the platform accessible with adaptive and assistive technology?

There are many helpful sites and resources that check accessibility, however, the most productive is user testing because users can find more than automated systems can.

WebAIM (Web Accessibility in Mind) features many tools and resources to create accessible web pages including the *Color Contrast Checker*, which checks color contrast on websites. The *Tota11y Accessibility Visualization Toolkit* is a plug-in that inserts a button in the toolbar in your browser and displays accessibility errors on your page. The plug-in detects images with no alt-text, links with incorrect labels, color contrast issues and more. *WAVE, the Web Accessibility Evaluation Tool,* is a suite of evaluation tools that identify accessibility and WCAG errors.

Economic Accessibility

Another form of accessibility is being unable to use something because of the lack of resources, money, and privilege. People may not be able to afford an Internet connection or technical equipment, and thus cannot attend and benefit from web programs. These barriers, often called the *digital divide,* also need addressing. Think about how your organization can aid Internet accessibility issues, give more access to low-income families, keep programming inclusive, and help bridge the digital divide.

Many of our patrons use libraries because of access issues. The American Library Association acknowledges this disproportionate impact the digital divide has on low-income families, rural residents, tribal communities, African Americans, Latinos, and people with disabilities and affirms the need for universal broadband access.[7]

Librarians can act as advocates at their organization and legal level and contact state representatives for additional funding, advocate for wireless hotspots, offline documents, and partnerships with businesses for increased accessibility. Tips for inclusion include set times and conditions for the broadest potential audiences, asking in advance about accessibility, creating ground rules, and asking audience members for feedback. Partnerships with hospitals, food banks, little free libraries, local radio and television stations, and schools can help libraries reach more users. In order for librarians to connect families with resources, they need to consider each community's unique interests and needs. Think about the community groups served or potentially served by the library and what resources are or are not accessible.

Key Points

- Accessibility covers various kinds of disabilities, visible or not.
- Economic accessibility ensures that resources and services are affordable and available for all.
- Do everything you can to make your content clear and accessible for all users.
- Many third-party applications and devices are available to assist participants with technology. Make sure your resources are compatible with these devices.

Notes

1. "Introduction to Understanding WCAG 2.0," Introduction to Understanding WCAG 2.0 | Understanding WCAG 2.0, accessed October 29, 2021, https://www.w3.org/TR/UNDERSTANDING-WCAG20/intro.html.

2. "Assistive Technology Act of 1998," Assistive Technology Act of 1998 | Section508.gov, accessed October 1, 2021, https://web.archive.org/web/20160329151743/http://www.section508.gov/assistive-technology-act-1998.

3. "Digital Accessibility Resources," MOPD, accessed October 1, 2021, www1.nyc.gov/site/mopd/resources/digital-accessibility-guides.page.

4. "About DCMP," The Described and Captioned Media Program, accessed August 22, 2021, https://dcmp.org/about-dcmp.

5. "Semantic Structure: Regions, Headings, and Lists," WebAIM, accessed October 1, 2021, https://webaim.org/techniques/semanticstructure/#contentstructure.

6. "Semantic Structure: Regions, Headings, and Lists," WebAIM, accessed October 1, 2021, https://webaim.org/techniques/semanticstructure/#contentstructure.

7. Talia Evans, "Bridging the Digital Divide in the Age of COVID-19," Advocacy, Legislation & Issues, August 6, 2020, www.ala.org/advocacy/diversity/odlos-blog/digital-divide-partnerships.

CHAPTER 11

Putting It All Together

▷ Where do I go from here?

▷ How do I avoid burnout?

▷ How do I keep up with changing technology?

I COVERED A LOT OF INFORMATION in the last ten chapters and probably could continue for another hundred pages. By the time you are reading this book, a lot of the information may have already changed. But I hope I helped you create a forward-thinking foundation of approaching instruction through the technology point of view. I hope you are thinking about how you can make technology more accessible for all users.

Remember to be flexible, and think about how you can reach your population. Constantly learn from the past as you are thinking toward the future. Every program and session is a learning experience, and you can take attendees' reactions and responses as feedback to make your next session even better.

Actionable Steps

All this information can seem overwhelming, but I urge you to take a deep breath and remember that you need not do everything at once. Here are three actionable steps instructors can make depending on their roles.

High-level administration:

1. Ensure you have proper funds allocated for staffing, equipment, and licenses for online instruction.
2. Update or create your virtual programming policy, making sure it includes copyright and accessibility factors.

3. Evaluate what livestreaming services and platforms your organization uses and determine if it is time for any changes.

Supervisors:

1. Make sure that your staff receives proper training and support for online instruction.
2. Ensure your staff receives the proper support before, during, and after online instruction. This support involves help from other staff members during programs, and proper time, equipment, and space to put on a quality program.
3. Take time to watch your staff's programming and instruction and give them positive feedback and constructive criticism. And then take time to listen to your staff members' ideas and suggestions.

Online instructors:

1. Join a professional learning network and reach out and connect to someone from it. Then attend a program or class from another instructor in another state. See what you can learn from them.
2. Think about one tool you would like to try in a virtual program, test it out, and use it.
3. Talk to your attendees and get an idea about what they would like to try in a virtual program.

⟳ Roadblocks

I often find myself with the "conference high," where I am really excited about new ideas and cannot wait to try them out in the real world. Then when I return to work, my co-workers aren't quite as excited about my idea, my supervisor says they tried that a decade ago, and I'm so busy catching up on all the work I missed that I forget what my idea was in the first place.

Think about what is holding you back from trying the new idea and how you can work around that roadblock. Does your idea need slight modifications? Do you need to try collaborating with a different department? Do you need to allocate more time to this project? Once you clearly define the problem, then you can come up with a solution.

Did everyone stop coming to your virtual programming? Take time to think about why this response happened. Was the time of day favorable? Was this program or course usually popular? Was something else happening that day?

Did you bring back in-person programming and there's no time for virtual programming? Can you turn an in-person program into a hybrid program? Are you able to rotate if a program is held in person or virtually? Should you offer less in-person programming because there are more virtual options? Think about how you can achieve a balance. Not everything needs to go back to the way it used to be.

Are you burnt out with online instruction? Think about what frustrates you the most. Are there any ways you can stop those frustrations? Try taking a break from a certain program and trading with a coworker. See what you can modify to make it more interesting.

⊚ Changing Technology

New apps are invented every day, phones and computers are constantly receiving upgrades, and the onslaught of new technology never stops. As an information professional, it seems impossible to keep up with the ever-changing technology landscape. Just like with books, we are never going to have time to try or read everything. But that doesn't have to stop you from trying. Prioritize the technologies you want to test out and make time to try them. And from there find resources that work for you to keep up-to-date on technologies in your specific area. These resources include Twitter feeds, professional networks, library journals, Facebook groups, and even print magazines. Try to be selective about your interests, because remember you do not have time to read everything. It can be helpful to move beyond libraries and look at what technical industries and other organizations are doing. This way, you can learn about new content before everyone else.

Try signing up for new feature alerts and announcement emails from technology platforms like Google Cloud or Amazon Web Service. Keep an eye on the open-source community and follow tech news like WIRED, The Verge, and TechCrunch.

Chapter 8 categorizes and recommends technology resources. Search for those key words and filter by date to find the latest technologies. Or type in *substitute for* and an app that you are looking to replace. Chapter 8 also highlights library-specific networks and groups to learn about technology.

Conferences are also a great place to learn about new and emerging technologies because many vendors bring their technology to demonstrate. The first time I tried virtual reality was at an ALA Conference.

Library conferences specifically about technology include Code4Lib, an annual gathering of technologists from around the world who work for libraries and museums and have a commitment to open technologies. The conference Computers in Libraries Connect is produced by Information Today Inc. and is a virtual conference where information professionals from around the world share innovative ideas on the future of libraries. The conference advertises to a broad scope of librarians, which works well with the audience of this book. The ACM/IEEE-CS Joint Conference on Digital Libraries (JCDL) is an international forum that focuses on digital libraries and associated technical, practical, and social issues. Recommended disciplines include computer science, information science, librarianship, archival science and practice, museum studies and practice, technology, medicine, social sciences, and humanities, and people from all domains are welcome.

⊚ Ideas to Remember

After reading this book, I hope you remember these key concepts:

Online instruction is here to stay. It may require more work, but it is accessible to more patrons, the present and future of information sharing, and key to libraries maintaining their roles as leaders in sharing information.

Online instruction is everywhere. You don't need to be a licensed teacher or an instruction librarian to participate in online instruction. Librarians are constantly helping patrons, sharing information, and putting on presentations. The instruction is always there—the details simply change depending on the person.

Don't reinvent the wheel. I mentioned many ideas in this book and all of them and more were done in libraries and schools around the world. Reach out to people who have already tried these activities and learn from their experiences.

Pedagogy first, technology second. Don't get so lost in the glamor and glory of technology that you lose who you are as an instructor. When looking at technology, always consider how it can make the experience better for yourself and your attendees.

Establish organizational policies and standards. If your organization does not have policies, make them. If the policies need an update, update them. If you don't have the power to do so, show this book to your supervisor and tell them that you are concerned for the legal safety and image of your organization.

Take aspects of in-person programming and modify their best parts to the digital format. Remember that not everything needs to be the same, but not everything needs to be different either. Take time to practice and explore in the online environment.

Remember that digital programming takes more time. Preparation execution, promoting, filming, and editing adds many more layers to the programming experience. Calculate the time needed to do online programming and make sure that your organization has the time, staff, and resources to achieve your goals.

Don't turn into a computer. Human beings crave socialization and friendship. Just because programs are on computers doesn't mean that everything needs to be perfect and automated. Remember to insert yourself into programs and make them interactive and fun. This will keep viewers invested and engaged.

Keep up-to-date on copyright. Laws and permissions are constantly changing, and as a librarian, it is your responsibility to interpret and comply with copyright laws.

Bring your accessibility framework everywhere you go. Every decision, every program, every idea should have accessibility in mind. Because libraries are for everyone—and to keep that statement true—libraries need to be accessible.

There's not one way to go about leading online instruction. Find your style and determine what methods work best for you and your community. And don't hesitate to switch things up and modify (even in the middle of a program if you're comfortable with that).

Key Points

- Take an actionable step toward streamlining the online instruction process at your organization.
- Remember to be realistic in your goals and ideas for online instruction, but don't get disheartened.
- As technology evolves, so will online instruction. And librarianship will evolve along with it.

Bibliography

"About DCMP." The Described and Captioned Media Program. Accessed August 22, 2021. https://dcmp.org/about-dcmp.

"Assistive Technology Act of 1998." Assistive Technology Act of 1998 | Section508.gov. Accessed October 1, 2021. https://web.archive.org/web/20160329151743/http://www.section508.gov/assistive-technology-act-1998.

"Behind the Blackboard!" Accessed October 4, 2021. https://blackboard.secure.force.com/apex/publickbarticleview?id=kAA1O000000Kz2B&homepage=true.

Bond, Shannon. "A Pandemic Winner: How Zoom Beat Tech Giants to Dominate Video Chat." NPR, March 19, 2021. www.npr.org/2021/03/19/978393310/a-pandemic-winner-how-zoom-beat-tech-giants-to-dominate-video-chat.

Canvas Community. "What Are the Canvas Accessibility Standards?" Instructure Community, September 30, 2021. https://community.canvaslms.com/t5/Canvas-Basics-Guide/What-are-the-Canvas-accessibility-standards/ta-p/1564.

"Choosing Media Content for Young Children Using the E-AIMS Model." ZERO TO THREE. Accessed August 2, 2021. www.zerotothree.org/resources/2533-choosing-media-content-for-young-children-using-the-e-aims-model.

"Circular 15A Duration of Copyright." Copyright. Accessed October 2, 2021. www.copyright.gov/circs/circ15a.pdf.

"Classroom | Google for Education." Google Classroom. Google. Accessed November 3, 2021. https://edu.google.com/products/classroom/.

"Copyright Act of 1790: U.S. Copyright Office." Copyright Act of 1790 | U.S. Copyright Office. Accessed September 20, 2021. https://copyright.gov/about/1790-copyright-act.html.

"Copyright Term and the Public Domain in the United States." Copyright Information Center. Cornell. Accessed October 2, 2021. https://copyright.cornell.edu/publicdomain.

"Digital Accessibility Resources." MOPD. Accessed October 1, 2021. www1.nyc.gov/site/mopd/resources/digital-accessibility-guides.page.

"Distance Education Timeline." American Center for the Study of Distance Education. Accessed June 24, 2021. https://sites.psu.edu/acde/2019/02/02/distance-education-timeline/.

"Documentation." About Moodle—MoodleDocs. Accessed October 3, 2021. https://docs.moodle.org/311/en/About_Moodle.

Evans, Talia. "Bridging the Digital Divide in the Age of COVID-19." Advocacy, Legislation & Issues, August 6, 2020. www.ala.org/advocacy/diversity/odlos-blog/digital-divide-partnerships.

"The Evolution of Distance Learning." Florida National University, August 15, 2019. www.fnu.edu/evolution-distance-learning/.

Ewagner. "Copyright: Distance Education and the Teach Act." Advocacy, Legislation & Issues. American Library Association, March 10, 2019. www.ala.org/advocacy/copyright/teachact/distanceeducation.

Fowler, Clara, Carla Wilson Buss, Chad Kahl, and Susan Vega Garica. "Standards for Proficiencies for Instruction Librarians and Coordinators: A Practical Guide." American Library Association. Association of College and Research Libraries, June 24, 2007. www.ala.org/acrl/sites/ala.org.acrl/files/content/standards/profstandards.pdf.

García-Morales, Víctor J., Aurora Garrido-Moreno, and Rodrigo Martín-Rojas. "The Transformation of Higher Education after the COVID Disruption: Emerging Challenges in an Online Learning Scenario." Frontiers, February 11, 2021. www.frontiersin.org/articles/10.3389/fpsyg.2021.616059/full.

Garrison, D. Randy, Terry Anderson, and Walter Archer. "Critical Inquiry in a Text-Based Environment: Computer Conferencing in Higher Education." *The Internet and Higher Education* 2, no. 2–3 (1999): 87–105. https://doi.org/10.1016/s1096-7516(00)00016-6.

Hein, George E. "CECA (International Committee of Museum Educators) Conference: Constructivist Learning Theory." In *Exploratorium*. Accessed September 12, 2021. www.exploratorium.edu/education/ifi/constructivist-learning.

Howell, Lily. "One Year on, Is Zoom Safe to Use?" Growth Through Technology, March 19, 2021. www.netitude.co.uk/blog/one-year-on-is-zoom-safe-to-use.

"Introduction to Understanding WCAG 2.0." Introduction to Understanding WCAG 2.0 | Understanding WCAG 2.0. Accessed October 29, 2021. www.w3.org/TR/UNDERSTANDING-WCAG20/intro.html.

"Leep Online." School of Information Sciences. Accessed November 1, 2021. https://ischool.illinois.edu/degrees-programs/ms-library-and-information-science/mslis-leep-online.

Maslow, Abraham H. *A Theory of Human Motivation*. Radford, VA: Wilder Publications, 2018.

Mayer, Richard E. *Multimedia Learning*. Cambridge, UK: Cambridge University Press, 2020.

"Media and Children." American Academy of Pediatrics. Accessed September 2, 2021. www.aap.org/en/patient-care/media-and-children/.

Morgan, Chris, and Meg O'Reilly. *Assessing Open and Distance Learners*. London: Kogan Page, 1999.

"The Most Comprehensive K-12 Teaching and Learning Suite." Schoology. Accessed October 3, 2021. www.schoology.com/k-12.

November, Alan. "Crafting a Vision for Empowered Learning and Teaching: Beyond the $1,000 Pencil." November Learning, November 5, 2018. https://novemberlearning.com/article/crafting-vision-empowered-learning-teaching-beyond-1000-pencil/.

Ostman, Sarah. "Online Story Time & Coronavirus: It's Fair Use, Folks." Programming Librarian. ALA Public Programs Office, April 30, 2020. https://programminglibrarian.org/articles/online-story-time-coronavirus-it%E2%80%99s-fair-use-folks.

Paciga, Katie A., and Chip Donohue. "Technology and Interactive Media for Children." Fred Rogers Center. Accessed October 7, 2021. www.fredrogerscenter.org/wp-content/uploads/2017/07/Technology-and-Interactive-Media-for-Young-Children.pdf.

Palloff, Rena M., and Keith L. Pratt. *Building Online Learning Communities: Effective Strategies for the Virtual Classroom*. San Francisco: Jossey-Bass Publishers, 2007.

"Performance Measurement: Introduction to Project Outcome." Public Library Association (PLA), January 22, 2021. www.ala.org/pla/data/performancemeasurement.

"Prof Robert Kelly Is Back & This Time His Wife . . ." YouTube. Accessed September 1, 2021. www.youtube.com/watch?v=PLMSoD1riE0.

Proffitt, Merrilee, ed. *Leveraging Wikipedia: Connecting Communities of Knowledge*. Chicago: ALA Editions, the American Library Association, 2018.

Ray, Dr. Kecia. "Updating Bloom's Taxonomy for Digital Learning." TechLearning Magazine. Tech & Learning, February 16, 2021. www.techlearning.com/news/updating-blooms-taxonomy-for-digital-learning.

"Semantic Structure: Regions, Headings, and Lists." WebAIM. Accessed October 1, 2021. https://webaim.org/techniques/semanticstructure/#contentstructure.

Sumner, Jennifer. "Serving the System: A Critical History of Distance Education." *Open Learning: The Journal of Open, Distance and e-Learning* 15, no. 3 (2000): 267–85. https://doi.org/10.1080/713688409.

"The Teach Act." Accessed October 2, 2021. www.copyright.com/wp-content/uploads/2015/04/CR-Teach-Act.pdf.

U.S. Copyright Office. "The Music Modernization Act." The Music Modernization Act | U.S. Copyright Office. Accessed October 15, 2021. www.copyright.gov/music-modernization/.

Wenger, Etienne. *Communities of Practice: Learning, Meaning, and Identity.* Cambridge, UK: Cambridge University Press, 2018.

"What's Wrong?" Flippity.net. Accessed October 28, 2021. www.flippity.net/WhatsWrong.htm.

Index

About the Author

Emily Rose Mroczek (Bayci) is a freelance children's librarian in the Chicago suburbs. She received a bachelor's degree in journalism and a master's degree in library and information science from the University of Illinois at Urbana-Champaign.

The author interned in the Frank Giamatti Research Center at the Baseball Hall of Fame in Cooperstown, New York, and began her career as a children's librarian at the Cincinnati & Hamilton County Public Library before settling in the Chicago suburbs.

Emily focuses on bridging the digital divide and online learning. Her experience includes working as a help desk and instructional design assistant for the iSchool at the University of Illinois at Urbana-Champaign. In her final graduate project, she designed computer labs for churches in low-income communities.

She currently substitutes at local libraries, provides online instruction, and co-leads the *Heavy Medal* blog for *School Library Journal*.

Outside of libraries, Emily enjoys playing with her baby and toddler, adult storytelling, and thinking of crafts she will make one day.